The Times, 1972: 'One feels that Uganda cannot afford General Amin's warm-hearted generosity.'

Lord Palmerston: 'Die, my dear doctor? That's the *last* thing I shall do.'

Gerald Ford: 'I say that if Lincoln were living today, he would turn over in his grave!'

Princess Anne, asked about a visit by Captain Mark Phillips, 1973: 'He is here solely to exercise the horses.'

Ian Smith, 1975: 'There are going to be no dramatic changes in Rhodesia.'

Don Atyeo, formerly a journalist in Australia, first teamed up with his co-author to compile the *Book of Sports Quotes*. Jonathon Green's past productions include the *Book of Rock Quotes*, *Famous Last Words* and a *Directory of Infamy*.

DON'T QUOTE ME

Compiled by
Don Atyeo & Jonathon Green

Cartoons by
Edward Barker

ARROW BOOKS

Arrow Books Limited
17-21 Conway Street, London W1P 6JD

An imprint of the Hutchinson Publishing Group

London Melbourne Sydney Auckland
Johannesburg and agencies throughout
the world

First published in Great Britain by
Hamlyn Paperbacks 1981
Fourth printing 1982
Arrow edition 1984

Printed and bound in Great Britain by
Anchor Brendon Limited, Tiptree, Essex

ISBN 0 09 937440 4

CONTENTS

INTRODUCTION

'He who laughs has not yet heard the bad news.' (Bertolt Brecht)

These are the *other* famous last words. The ones you may survive but more than likely wish you hadn't.

Ever since Adam ordered up an apple, foot-in-mouth disease has been epidemic among humans. 'I'm all right, Jack' we inform the world, just before it crashes on to our heads. Boastful, arrogant, at best ludicrously optimistic, we plunge gleefully into the pits of our own construction. None of us is immune.

Some are more prone to suffer than others. The politician, the entrepreneur, the sportsman, the soldier, in fact everyone who pokes their head above the parapet to shout 'I am the greatest!' can hardly expect our sympathy when it gets knocked off.

Or the false prophets, both professional and amateur. We'd all love to predict the future and everyone has a go. For everyone who actually makes their living out it, there must be a million who go it alone and, judging by results, with about the same chance of success. Or failure.

Or the critics, those self-appointed experts who offer their diktats to the world: planners, pundits, the whole range of 'opinion-makers' in every sphere. How often those lovingly presented opinions prove disastrously incorrect. All these people choose to play with fire. Who can resist a smile when they get singed?

Unfortunately, Fate needs no encouragement to deliver the

low blow. You don't have to predict the apocalypse for 4 am Tuesday week to come unstuck. After all, someone had to live next door to young Adolf, and maybe he really did seem a nice lad . . . And who hasn't come out with some appalling social gaffe that leaves you and your audience wincing with embarrassment. And then there's the ultimate, when death arrives to make a mockery of all that bedside bravado. 'Die, my dear doctor?' said Lord Palmerston, inches from the grave. 'That's the last thing I shall do.' Indeed it was.

However hard we try, no matter what we're doing, so often it all seems to end up the same sad way. Foot on the banana skin, pitched face down in the mire. 'I told you so', smirks Life. Not that we ever bother to listen.

Certainly it's all very funny. What's more satisfying than watching your neighbour smear egg on his face? Laugh if you must. It's irresistible. But laugh quietly, for there, but for the grace of this particular moment, go we all.

DON ATYEO
JONATHON GREEN

WHOOPS!

We would all like to be able to predict the future. For whatever the reason – health, wealth, fame, fortune or simply whether to take a mac or not – the possibility of looking ahead is infinitely alluring. And so we chance our various prophetic arms, stabbing into what has to be the dark with the optimistic hope of lighting up the way. So we gamble, and challenge the fates, the opposition or just the weather. And, as in most games of chance, the odds favour the house, so we usually lose. And then, like gamblers everywhere, we try again.

Bird Stretcher

In 1965 BOAC found that, due to some in-flight mishap, a housemartin called Bonzo, had been unable to join his fellows on the annual migration to Nigeria. A BOAC spokesperson traced Bonzo to the vet where he was recuperating and assured the press, 'We'll fly Bonzo back ourselves!' Waiting for embarkation at Heathrow, Bonzo was freed from his cage to perform a few spins for the cameras, upon which he promptly flew into a plate-glass window and broke his neck.

Springtime for Hitler

According to Beverley Nichols, a journalist, writing in the 1930s: 'Herr Hitler has one of the endearing characteristics of Ferdinand the Bull. Just when the crowds expect him to be most violent he stops and smells the flowers. I have a feeling, and I hope that I am right, that for the next month or so Herr Hitler is going to take things a little easier and smell the flowers and listen to the nightingales.'

Can't Add Up

An anonymous teacher once assured the future discoverer of relativity, then aged ten: 'Einstein, you will never amount to much.'

Slow to Bloom

Unable to read until the age of eight, G. K. Chesterton was perennially bottom of his class. 'If we could open your head, we should not find any brain but only a lump of white fat', remarked one exasperated master. Chesterton went on to become one of England's most popular and successful novelists.

The young Charles Darwin, destined to overturn conventional biology with his *The Origin of Species*, was another problem pupil. 'You care for nothing but shooting, dogs and rat-catching, and you will be a disgrace to yourself and all your family', his father railed.

His first teacher called him 'addled', his father dismissed him as 'a dunce', and his school headmaster wrote that he 'would never make a success of anything'. It was only after his mother took him under her wing that Thomas Edison began to show signs that he would one day 'invent' the modern world, patenting over a thousand inventions including the electric light bulb and the gramophone.

The young James Watt was labelled 'dull and inept' by his school masters and bullied unmercifully by his fellow pupils. It was not until he had invented the steam engine and laid the foundations of the Industrial Revolution that his genius was fully recognized.

Going Down?

Joseph P. Kennedy, Ambassador to Britain in 1939, opined: 'I have yet to talk to any military or naval expert of any nationality who thinks, with the present and prospective set-up of England and France on one side and Germany and Russia and their potential allies on the other, that England has a Chinaman's chance . . . England and France can't quit, whether they would like to or not, and I am convinced because I live here that England will go down fighting.'

Kennedy was withdrawn as ambassador soon afterwards.

Horse Feathers

In 1896 inventor Henry Ford first demonstrated his new automobile. As he drove the weird contraption, crowds gathered to laugh, jeer and shout: 'Get a horse!' In 1909 Ford offered his Model T for sale for just $850 (down to $240 by 1924), and the world lurched into the automotive age.

Birth of a Notion

Whatever he achieved as a director, Hollywood pioneer D. W. Griffith (*Intolerance, Birth of a Nation*), was rather less talented as a clairvoyant. In 1924 he predicted: 'In the year 2024 the most important single thing which the cinema will have helped in a large way to accomplish will be that of eliminating from the face of the civilized world all armed conflict. With the use of the universal language of moving pictures the true meaning of the brotherhood of man will have been established throughout the earth. The Englishman will have learned that the soul of the Japanese is, essentially, the same as his own. The Frenchman will realize that the American's ideals are his ideals. All men are created equal.'

We're Oil Confident

In 1965, a 'highly-placed and distinguished economist' was quoted in the press as saying: 'There is only one thing about which we can be absolutely certain in the future – and that is the continued supply of cheap petroleum from the Middle East.'

Brief Encounter

Iranian Foreign Minister Sadegh Ghotzbadeh, interviewed in *Time* magazine, April 7, 1980: 'Frankly, a resolution of the hostage problem is imperative within two months . . . I expect the problem to be resolved in two months or so . . .?

Briefer Encounter

In 1974 an impoverished miner's son delighted the world's gossip columns when he told them of his impending marriage to millionairess Rachel Fitler, an eccentric older woman: 'Rachel and I are going to be married at Christmas and later on we are going on a three-month honeymoon cruise.' But later that day, when the confident swain appeared at Miss Fitler's front door, her butler threw him out.

Pish Off!

At 2am on September 13, 1666, an anxious watchman summoned the Lord Mayor of London to see a fire that had begun in a bakery in Pudding Lane (in the City). The Lord Mayor glanced at the flames and declared, 'Pish! A woman might piss it out', and retired to his bed.

The flames developed into the Great Fire of London, devastating 300 acres, 13,000 houses, 87 parish churches and most of the City's major buildings. Six months later cellars were still smouldering. Miraculously only eight people died in the fire.

Refurbished

Wilhelm Reich, renegade student of Freud and pioneer of the orgone box, declared in 1946: 'In the course of thirty years the human race will have been biologically restored; it will come into the world without any trace of fascist distortion.'

Winning Grovel

Tony Greig, then England's cricket captain, predicted in 1976 that his team could beat the West Indies in that summer's tour. After all, 'These West Indians, when they're on top they're magnificent, but when they're down they grovel.' The enraged West Indians took their opponents apart in the series, and Viv Richards, their star batsman, scored two double-centuries.

Vemarana for a Day

In May 1980, 800 Melanesians, some armed with clubs, bows and arrows, took over the largest island in the tropical New Hebrides, Espiritu Santo. They proclaimed independence from the New Hebrides' joint colonial overlords – Great Britain and France – and renamed the island Vemarana. At the head of the provisional government was 58-year-old former bulldozer driver Jimmy Stevens. Stevens established an office in a disused dancing academy and there he greeted the world's media. 'Time is not important here. We shall be open for business in a few days. We want to be free to make our own decisions, to run our economy and to have a picnic when we feel like having one. ' Vemarana lasted just eight weeks. Stevens was arrested, tried for his rebellion and jailed for fourteen years.

Dewey Eyed

On US election night, November 2, 1948, the *Chicago Tribune* was so sure of the result that they printed a first-edition headline before the results were known: 'Dewey Defeats Truman'. The morning, however, told otherwise. Harry Truman beat Governor Thomas E. Dewey by 303 electoral votes to 189 and by 24,179,345 to 21,991,291 popular votes.

Just the Job

Sir Gerald Nabarro, MP, commenting (in 1962) on the idea that Edward Heath might ever become Prime Minister: 'The

British public would never stomach a bachelor at 10 Downing Street.'

Over the Top

Margaret Thatcher, interviewed in the *Sunday Telegraph* on October 26, 1969, after her appointment as Shadow Spokesman on Education: 'No woman in my time will be Prime Minister or Chancellor or Foreign Secretary – not the top jobs. Anyway, I wouldn't want to be Prime Minister; you have to give yourself 100 per cent.'

Prodigal Son

In December 1973, *Esquire* magazine ran a list of the 'Ten Safest Cities in the United States', compiled by David Franke. Cited as No. 7 was Provo, Utah, for among other things, its 'ambitious youth programme that has apparently paid off'.

Three years later Gary Gilmore came home to Provo, having volunteered himself for capital punishment by firing squad after shooting dead two other Provo citizens.

Weather Man

In 1964, the Director of the Provincial Weather Bureau in Formosa publicly forecast: 'Hurricane Gloria will not strike Taiwan.'

But it did, the next day, killing 239 people and causing $17 million in damage. Accused of negligence, arrested, charged and tried, the hapless director claimed in court that he had tried his best. The case was adjourned indefinitely.

This Sporting Life

Sport, theoretically based on luck as well as judgment, defeats commentators, competitors and consumers alike.

The BBC's radio commentator for the 1938 FA Cup Final, Lieutenant-Commander Tommy Woodroffe, at one point promised his listeners: 'If there's a goal now, I'll eat my hat!' There was and he did.

In 1974, fresh from bringing once lowly Brighton into English soccer's first division, Brian Clough (formerly a star player himself) was hired by Leeds United to replace the veteran success Don Revie, who had recently moved to run the national squad. Clough told the press: 'I'm delighted to be going to Leeds as a manager. It is an exciting opportunity. I don't foresee any problems.'

His opportunity lasted just 44 disastrous days. He was then paid off, and Leeds continued to decline. Clough, on the other hand, prospers still elsewhere.

Phil Wrigley, American baseball club owner, pooh-poohed an innovation in the game as 'just a fad, a passing fancy'. However, night baseball turned out to be an instant success and remains a staple of the US game.

Stanley Matthews, soccer's future 'Wizard of Dribble', debuted aged just 17. A local soccer writer pronounced: 'Stanley Matthews lacks the big match temperament. He will never hold down a regular first-team place in top-class soccer.'

In 1974 Daley Thompson was practising his decathlon events. His coach, Tom McNab, informed him: 'You're a bum runner and you'll never make a decathlete.' Six years later Thompson won the Olympic Decathlon gold medal.

Zaire, October 30, 1974. Muhammad Ali vs George Foreman for the Heavy-weight boxing Championship of the World. Billed as 'The Rumble in the Jungle', the purses were large, the media contingent massive and the bally-hoo unrelenting. In the eighth round BBC commentator Harry Carpenter regaled his public: 'That's it. There's no way Ali can win this one now . . .'

At this point Ali, with a flurry of deadly jabs to Foreman's head, knocked his opponent out.

Let Them Eat Cake (1)

As Russia collapsed into revolution around her, the Czarina Alexandra showed fine hauteur. Writing to her husband Nicholas II, she typified the revolutionaries as 'youngsters and girls' who ran around shouting that they had no bread.

'They do this just to create some excitement. If the weather were cold they would probably all be staying at home. But the thing will pass and quiet down . . .'

Two days later she wrote again to the Czar: 'The whole trouble comes from . . . idlers, well-dressed people, wounded soldiers, high school girls, etc.' The 'real people' – cabbies, tram-drivers and the like, although on strike, were all for the Czar, 'because they worship you'.

According to another missive: 'Monday I read another scurrilous proclamation, but I think everything will be all right. The sun is shining so brightly and I feel so calm and at peace.' This was on the very eve of the Revolution, and the mob was at that moment forming outside the Winter Palace.

Wishful Thinking

Leon Trotsky, 1925: 'England is at last ripe for revolution.'

Keep Taking the Pills . . .

As President, General Eisenhower naturally had on call the finest medical expertise available. One night he seemed ill. His wife Maimie summoned Ike's personal physician, Howard Snyder, Surgeon-General of the US Army. He checked over his patient and assured Mrs Eisenhower that it was 'just indigestion, Maimie. Give him some bicarbonate.'

Yet, the President's illness persisted, not surprising considering that he had actually suffered a heart attack.

Future Shock

Clark Kerr, the Chancellor of the University of California, in 1959 forecast the 1960s: 'The employers are going to love this generation. They aren't going to press many grievances.

They are going to be easy to handle. There aren't going to be any riots.'

In January 1970, Haynes Johnson, reporter on the *Washington Post*, also reviewed the possibilities of a new decade: 'It is not the past that beckons us now; as the young people like to remind us, we are approaching the dawning of a new age, the age of Aquarius. Harmony and understanding, peace on earth and universal brotherhood are its heralds. At least, it's an optimistic omen.'

Dud Czech

The hapless Alexander Dubcek, architect of the 'Prague Spring' of 1968, returned from a meeting in Moscow on August 2nd to announce: 'I was asked at the airport whether our sovereignty was jeopardized and I am saying frankly that it is not.

Days later the Russian tanks invaded and Dubcek returned to Moscow in chains.

With Friends Like This . . .

Lord Beaverbrook, the press magnate, was asked in 1932 whether he wished to employ Winston Churchill, then an out-of-favour maverick, on the *Daily Express:* Why Churchill? He's a busted flush!'

After the war, Beaverbrook predicted the results of the 1945 General Election: 'I am convinced that Mr Churchill will carry his party to victory.' Churchill, was, of course, roundly defeated.

Class Clown

On May 13, 1970, National Guardsmen shot and killed four students at Kent State University in Ohio. Secretary of the Interior Walter Hickel wrote to President Nixon, worrying about the affair. An aide replied: 'Cool it Wally, this thing will blow over in 24 hours.' In fact, US campuses erupted.

Hard Times

Edward Heath, addressing the nation as Prime Minister in 1974: 'I intend to see to it that you have a Government that is capable of leading the country through the difficult times ahead.' He then called a General Election for February 1974, in which the public chose to replace him with a Labour Government.

Let Them Eat Cake (2)

Like all revolutions, the Russian one of 1917 was greeted by those in power the world over with the fervent wish that it would go away. Perhaps it was assumed that if one hoped and wrote hard enough, the revolutionaries really would vanish. Newspaper headlines of the time in England included *The Times* (December 11, 1916): 'Russia Firm and United' and the *Manchester Guardian* (November 24, 1917): 'The Bolsheviks Must Fall'. The Russian Prince Kropotkin, in describing the Bolshevik Revolution in 1920, observed: 'In my opinion the attempt to build up a Communist Republic on the lines of a strongly centralized State Communism, under the iron rule of a party, is ending in failure.'

Comrades in Arms

Chinese Premier Chou En Lai, affirming Marx's theories of world proletarian fraternity in 1965: 'We are firmly convinced that no force whatsoever can disrupt the great unity between the Chinese and the Soviet Peoples.'

THE LUNATIC FRINGE

The English genius, we are told, is eccentricity. A brief survey of the rest of the world proves, however, that such pleasures are by no means an Anglo-Saxon prerogative.

This is My Body

In 1976 Trans World Airlines (TWA) based their advertising on a new slogan: 'TWA is the only airline offering a choice of meals. You'll find a choice of three meals in coach, five in first class . . . You can choose between a full meal or a light snack . . .'

Passenger Lewis Pangbourne, however, obviously took this literally. Somewhere between Heathrow and JFK Airport he bit three of his fellow passengers 'because they scorned Jesus at a height of thirty thousand feet'. The airline subsequently reconsidered their campaign.

Sisterhood is Powerful

Addressing his audience in the *Berliner Tageblatt* on July 12, 1914, Professor Hans Friedenthal of Berlin University stated his opinions on the evolution of 'the new woman' in an era of suffragism and higher education. 'Brain work will cause her to become bald, while increasing masculinity and contempt for beauty will induce the growth of hair on the face. In the future, therefore, women will be bald and will wear long moustaches and patriarchal beards.'

The March of Science

Dr John Lightfoot, then Vice Chancellor of Cambridge University, shortly prior to the publication of Charles

Darwins' *The Origin of Species* in 1859, stated unequivocally: 'Heaven and Earth were created altogether at the same instant on October 23, 4004 BC, at 9 o'clock in the morning.'

This was in the great tradition of a scientific predecessor, Scipio Chiaramonti, who had said: 'Animals, which move, have limbs and muscles. The earth does not have limbs or muscles. Therefore it does not move.'

Fear of Frying

On September 26, 1830, Colonel Robert Gibbon Johnson stood on the steps of the courthouse in Salem, Massachusetts with a basket of tomatoes and challenged a 2000-strong crowd. The superstitious Puritans eschewed the plant, accepting it as an ornamental bush but refusing utterly to eat the 'love apples', which were seen at best as a vile aphrodisiac and more likely as a poison that would turn blood to acid. Johnson would attempt to eat the entire basket – and survive. His own doctor, James van Metter, harangued the crowd. 'The foolish colonel will foam and froth at the mouth and double over with appendicitis. All that oxalic acid, one dose, and you're dead! If the Wolf Peach (sic) is too ripe and warmed by the sun, he'll be exposing himself to brain fever. Should he, by some unlikely chance, survive, I must warn him that the skin . . . will stick to his stomach and cause cancer.'

The crowd waited breathlessly as Johnson, wearing black, ascended the steps and took up the first tomato. The hysterical screams turned to cheers as he worked his way through the entire basket, and van Metter slipped prudently away.

Buffalo Bull

Marvin Redland, a guitar salesman from Norfolk, California, was drinking in his local bar and discussing reincarnation with the barmaid. 'I was a canary in a previous life', she insisted. 'In my next life I'll be a buffalo.' Redland laughed. 'You can laugh', said the girl, 'but I'll prove it.' With which she reached under the bar, produced a shotgun and blew off her own head. She failed to rematerialize as a buffalo, and Redland was arrested and charged with abetting a suicide.

The Outer Limits

UFOs, unidentified flying objects, continue to fascinate, even in the pragmatic space age of today. From Jimmy Carter, who said in 1976 'I am convinced UFOs exist, because I have seen one' to Lionel Beer, Managing Editor of *Spacelink*, a UFO magazine, who sweetly admitted 'Ours is a nuts and bolts organization', the interest never dies.

In Moneymore, Northern Ireland, on September 8, 1956, farmer Thomas J. Hutchinson told police, 'I captured a flying saucer, but it got away. It was bright red, with two dark red marks at the end and three dark red stripes. It had a saucer-shaped base.' The object appeared in a bog 200 yards from Hutchinson's farm kitchen and he and his wife went out to see it. When they came near the object it started to spin. 'I kicked it over, but it returned to its original position.' He then grabbed it, put a hammer lock on it, and started to carry it to the local police. 'I put the saucer down for a minute, and what do you think? It started to spin again.' Then it rose from the ground and vanished into the clouds. According to the local police, 'Thomas Hutchinson is a level-headed, God-fearing chap. He's not the sort of man who would imagine he seized a flying saucer if he didn't have one.' An RAF spokesman later identified the errant saucer as an escaped weather balloon.

In July 1963 another farmer, 71-year-old Roy Blanchard, backed by his neighbour, former space scientist Robert

Randall, claimed that a 600-ton spacecraft from Uranus had left an eight-foot-diameter crater in a Wiltshire field. 'My barley and potatoes just disappeared', said Blanchard, and he spoke of cows 'peeling' and the spacecraft, mounted on a 90-foot-high tripod, sucking produce from the field. Randall's wife, besieged by the press, stated: 'He's a doctor, and he knows what he's talking about.' The RAF, the Army, the media and a member of a London UFO organization converged on the farm in Tidworth, Wiltshire. Despite Dr Randall's opinion and Farmer Blanchard's protestations, they gave their verdict: the cows and the crops were suffering from mildew.

The more devoted UFO spotters often join the Aetherius Society, founded in 1954 by a London cabbie named George King who in May of that year had heard a musical voice tell him, as he did his washing, 'You are to become the voice of Interplanetary Parliament.' King has since applied to join the UN as a delegate from Venus.

In September 1967 six supposed UFOs appeared across a 220-mile swathe of English countryside. They were all bleeping, gunmetal-coloured and highly mysterious. One appeared on a Bromley golf course, one in an Ascot potato field, one in a ploughed field at Newbury, and others at Clivedon, Chippenham and the Isle of Sheppey. The six made an almost perfectly straight line from the Bristol Channel to the Thames Estuary. Senior police officers who inspected the 'saucers' stated: 'This is too much of a coincidence to be a hoax.'

The Army was summoned and a bomb squad crew promptly exploded the specimen they were offered. Another was being carefully transported by helicopter to RAF Manston when it dropped and burst, revealing a load of what seemed remarkably like pigswill. Eventually the truth was admitted. The 'UFOs' had been built by students at Farnborough Technical College as a rag week stunt for charity.

In September 1968 Buenos Aires was gripped by rumours that a flying saucer had landed on one of the motorways that ring the city. One witness said, 'The thing crashed into a car and two bald-headed dwarfs emerged. They were arrested by local air-force authorities.' Hundreds of people flocked to the highway when the news was broadcast. Two casino workers swore that no less than five aliens were at large. They described how the 'humanoids' had made 'wierd inscriptions on our car with something that looked like a welding torch'. They also told how the aliens had paralyzed them and taken blood samples from their fingertips. Others claimed to have seen the aliens carrying something like 'a portable TV set' through the city streets. The panic was compounded when Vittorio Corradi, the Vice President of the Mendoza Space Centre, said: 'There is no doubt that beings from outer space have communicated with us.'

Yet in the end, the reports proved a hoax. The first stories had been faked, and then later excitement grew genuinely. The Argentine Government swiftly passed a law making anyone spreading such rumours in the future liable to be jailed.

The Nun's Story

Sidney Perk's girlfriend threatened to break off their relationship. 'Unless you learn what it is like to be a woman'. In September 1975 Mr Perk was arrested walking up Florence Nightingale Walk robed as a nun. In court WPC Mary Roberts explained that she had suspected the transvestite Sister because 'it was the first time I had ever seen a nun in wedge heels'.

High Times

Dr Richard Alpert, cohort of LSD guru Timothy Leary and soon to be renamed Baba Ram Dass, speaking in 1967: 'In about seven or eight years the psychedelic population will be able to vote anybody into office that they want to. Allen Ginsberg? Sure. Imagine what it would be like to have anyone in high political office within our understanding of the universe. I mean, let's imagine that Bobby Kennedy had a fully expanded consciousness. Just imagine him, in his position, what he would be able to do.'

Take Me Now

In 1976 attendants at the General Hospital in Toulouse, France, were approached by a man who asked them, 'Can I donate my body to science?' On being informed by a porter that indeed he could, Paul Santon, a 77-year-old caretaker, produced a revolver and shot himself dead where he stood.

Breath Taking

From the *Gynaecology* of the Greek physician Soranus, published in AD 138, comes an allegedly foolproof method of contraception: The woman ought, in the moment during coitus when the man ejaculates his sperm, to hold her breath, draw her body back a little so that the semen cannot penetrate to the Os Uteri, then immediately get up and sit down with bent knees and, in this position, provoke sneezes.'

Nature Boy

Evangelist Larry Clayton was preaching to his congregation seated in a tent near Godfrey, Illinois, in 1973. He brandished a cross and told them: 'Jesus can calm the storm in your life, too!'

At this point a freak prairie storm ripped the tent from its moorings, hurled it 35 feet into the sky, shredded it into pieces and knocked down a nearby oak tree. Clayton commented: 'It was a miracle nobody was hurt.'

Stretcher Case

In September 1924 Sir Bruce Bruce-Porter spoke out against fashion innovation: 'Rubber corsets are a national danger. The girls of today pride themselves on getting rid of their mothers' Victorian corsets. They must beware lest they get into the worse bondage of the infernal band called the rubber corset.'

Deep-Sea Adventure

When Margate bathers spotted a pedalo far out to sea, a local constable set out to the rescue. As he approached the pedalo, the man in it shouted, 'I'm off to Amsterdam!' He then threw a bottle at the constable, hitting him on the head.

It was left to the five-man crew of the Margate lifeboat – bolstered by five more constables – to bring the offender ashore at Margate four hours later, handcuffed and lashed to a stretcher.

Sink or Swim

Brian Cottingham, a would-be daredevil, and Grimsby night-club manager, announced that he intended to jump the 37 feet off Cleethorpes Pier to raise money for the Variety Club of Great Britain. This magnanimous gesture was somewhat constrained when, on his arrival, he found that the tide was three-quarters of a mile out. Undeterred, Mr Cottingham, clad in a yellow crash helmet, pink water wings and an 1890s bathing costume, waved bravely, shouted 'The show must go on!' and jumped. Interviewed later in his hospital bed, Mr Cottingham expressed satisfaction that so large a crowd had turned out.

Out of His Depth

In July 1955 Lord Noel-Buxton declared his intention to walk across the River Thames at a specific spot to prove a theory concerning a ford. A supporter, Anthony Carlisle, wrote to the *Spectator* magazine, citing his lordship as a 'sensitive student of history prepared to test his theories about Roman fords at considerable discomfort and even risk'. On the appointed day Lord Noel-Buxton set out but sank almost immediately. Afterwards he commented on the unexpectedly deep water: 'It must be all that rain up in the Cotswolds.'

Mysterious Ways

Speaking in 1966, American prelate Bishop Fulton J. Sheen announced: 'Spiritually, radio and television are beautiful examples of the inspired wisdom of the ages. Radio is like the Old Testament, inasmuch as it is the hearing of wisdom without seeing it. TV is like the New Testament, because in it the wisdom becomes flesh and dwells among us.'

Major Sacrifice

Major Arthur Corbett-Smith, a 65-year-old author and former BBC official, held strong views on the old. All sixty-year-olds 'whose continued existence does not in some measure benefit the community' should be consigned 'to the lethal chamber'. In 1945 the Major proved a man of his word. Covering his head with a Union Jack, he shot hiimself dead on Margate Promenade. A letter, headed 'Corbett-Smith on his self-dispatch', was read out at the inquest.

The Rich Are Different

In early 1975 one Richard Scholes appeared at a Herfordshire auctioneers to bid successfully, for the vacant 2,435-acre De Trafford Estate. Closing out the bidding at £2,450,000, Scholes told the auctioneer, 'I've forgotten my chequebook'. A sheaf of blanks was instantly proffered and he blithely signed one. It bounced. Arrested shortly afterwards, Scholes told police, 'I have become extremely rich, a millionaire several times over. I own two Rolls Royces and am awaiting delivery of another.' Why the mansion? 'I am going into politics and will need a house near London.' Scholes was jailed for four years for what the judge called 'a crackbrained scheme.'

Be Practical

In 1919, on the eve of America's 'Great Experiment' making the consumption of alcohol illegal, hellfire preacher Billy Sunday promised his flock: 'When we get Prohibition, the problem of what to do with farm surplus will be solved in a jiffy. The children of drunkards will consume this surplus in the form of flapjacks for breakfast.'

God's Helpers

The Bishop of Woolwich told his congregation in 1924: 'The use of all artificial contrivances [for contraception] is clearly opposed to Christian conduct. The sex instinct is a sacramental thing.'

Thirty years later the Archbishop of Canterbury offered his mite to the struggle against commercial television: 'For the sake of our children, we must resist it!'

In July 1925 the Charleston, a zany American dance, arrived in London. Inevitably the God-fearing , spearheaded by the clergy, were outraged. The Vicar of St Aidan's, Bristol, epitomized their terror: 'Any lover of the beautiful will die rather than be associated with the Charleston. It is neurotic! It is rotten! It stinks! Phew, open the windows.' Unfortunately, the country's premier trend-setter, the Prince of Wales, loved the dance, and soon the whole country was kicking up its feet delightedly.

In 1890 the bicycle boom hit America. One clergyman sprang to the attack. 'You cannot serve God', he said, 'and skylark on a bicycle'.

Blind Faith

Buster Sheary, an American college basketball coach, was trying to whip up his players' fervour during a tough game. Repeatedly smashing his head against a locker door, he screamed, 'It doesn't hurt! It doesn't hurt!' Seconds later Sheary had knocked himself out cold.

Elementary . . .

Sir Arthur Conan Doyle, for all the methodology of his famous fictional detective Sherlock Holmes, was much taken with the spirit world. As well as holding his own seances he found, on a journey to Yorkshire in 1920, a pair of young girls who not only claimed that they had seen 'real fairies' but had photographed them as well. 'The two little girls are absolutely honest', he wrote to R. D. Blumenfeld, Editor of the *Daily Express*. 'The episode will prove to be the start of a new era.' Blumenfeld was unimpressed and called Conan Doyle 'either a charlatan, a fool, a lunatic or a child'. The author's book, called *The Coming of the Fairies*, was not a success either.

Self-Delusion

D. H. Lawrence, that pioneer of fleshly delights, wrote in his *Pornography and Obscenity* in 1930: 'Masturbation is certainly the most dangerous sexual vice that a society can be afflicted with, in the long run.'

For Their Own Good

Field Magazine, 1978: 'Stopping otter hunting is unlikely to benefit otters.'

Homeward Bound

In 1978 an anonymous man approached Mrs Barbara East-man, a flower-seller in Naysmith Square, Mt St Bruno, Canada. He told her, 'I am God. Could you direct me to the nearest church, please?' Mrs Eastman offered directions. The man raised his hat, thanked her, and stepped into the road, only to be knocked down by a tractor and killed instantly. Police could not identify the victim, although he possessed a singular tattoo – a fly imprinted on his left buttock.

LOVE AND MARRIAGE

Love and marriage go together, as we all know, like a horse and carriage. Unfortunately, this is the age of the internal combustion engine . . .

Chips to Go

It was a fairy-tale marriage. Erik Estrada, star of the *Chips* TV motorbike cop show, wedded Joyce Miller on November 25, 1979. Gazing lovingly into each other's eyes, they murmured sweet nothings for the press. 'I adore Joyce', said Erik. 'Every man should have a woman like her. We are both very, very happy.' Responded Joyce, 'Erik is the finest human being I know. There's so much happiness between us.' But by September 18, 1980, when Joyce lodged her divorce petition with the Los Angeles Superior Court, the fairy tale had turned into a nightmare. 'I was enmeshed in a web of lies and fantasy that Joyce created', stated Estrada. 'The lies started right from the beginning. The day we applied for the marriage license.' Miller claimed: 'Living with Erik was the most bizarre experience of my life. I went through hell and it's a wonder that I kept my sanity.' She elaborated the horrors in an eighteen-page petition, and summed up: 'Erik is a taker. He doesn't know how to give.'

Grecian Half Billion

Christina Onassis, heiress to her father Aristotle's $500 million shipping, financial and industrial empire, has had problems finding 'Mr Right'. Her first marriage, at the age of 20, was to Los Angeles real estate broker Joseph Bolker, well the other side of 40. That lasted nine months.

The next came in 1975, four months after her father's demise, to fellow Greek Alexander Andreadis, scion of another Athens business family. Gushed the lucky man, 'It's like being made a king for life.' Well, not quite for life. The marriage collapsed in divorce two years later.

Then Christina moved on to her strangest choice yet: 37-year-old shipping agent Sergei Kauzov. The Russian-born Sergei took his new bride off to live with him in Moscow as the Onassis board of directors rocked in their seats. Christina looked around her new home in a dingy Moscow apartment and told the eager press: 'I can live here. I'm very adaptable.' But not *that* adaptable. This time the divorce cost Christina an oil tanker.

Poor Prospects

When Frederic Chopin proposed to Maria Wodzinska in 1836, Maria's mother approved but her father, Count Wincenty Wodzinski, quickly vetoed the engagement. *'No , a thousand times no!'* he thundered, repelled by the young composer's humble origins and poor physique. 'If at least he had better health and a little ambition!'

Just Good Friends

Hollywood syndicated columnist Earl Wilson wrote in September 1968: 'We think we can tell you with comparative assurance that Aristotle Onassis is not likely to be marrying Jackie Kennedy or anyone else. "Ari" had a drink or two with Maria [Callas] just before she flew back to Paris yesterday. The night before he had dinner with Jackie. He feels he's "not worthy of either of them". His friends are a little offended that columnists keep harping on his friendship with Jackie, trying to make a romance out of it; their family friendship goes back several years . . .'

Two weeks later 'Ari' and 'Jackie' announced their engagement.

Going Swimmingly

Daily Mail, August 7, 1970: 'Barbara Stonehouse, wife of the Labour Minister of Posts . . . assures me she has been looking younger and younger for the last twenty years "and I put that down to having a good husband".

Evening Standard, January 1971. Ann Sharpley wrote: 'There are some marriages that are so ideal and easy looking that you wonder why the rest of us can't manage it too. It's something to do with being each other's match and equal, of keeping together so that half isn't left behind, and maintaining some secret balance and link between the two – hard to define but immediately recognizable when you meet it. Barbara and John Stonehouse have always seemed to me to be married in that way.'

On November 21, 1974, John Stonehouse vanished, presumed drowned, from Miami Beach, Florida. He surfaced a year later in Australia with his secretary Sheila Buckley. Stonehouse was later jailed for fraud, and Mrs Stonehouse has divorced her husband.

Short and Sweet

A couple approached the bench in Nashville, Tennessee, where sat Judge Charles Galbreath one day in 1974. 'Can we keep the ceremony short?' they asked him. 'Do you want to get married?' he asked them. 'Yes'. 'You are'.

Flaming Row

In June 1965 George Baxter and his wife Delia were having a row. After a quarrelsome evening out, George left to take the babysitter home, saying as he left, 'When I get back I will show you something.' He returned, went straight onto the verandah behind their flat, then called his wife. She watched, too shocked to do more than say 'Don't be silly, George', as her husband up-ended a can of petrol over himself and lit a match. He died in flames.

Only Skin Deep

In March 1971 Ralph Smith prepared for a first night of marital bliss with his new young wife Christine Brown, of Royston, Hertfordshire. The blushing bride was slightly surprised to find that her husband chose to enter the marriage bed with both arms swathed in sticking plaster. Inevitably she asked him why. He mumbled an excuse, but Christine was adamant. She pulled off the plaster. Underneath Smith's arms were festooned with tattoos. Among other messages were 'True love to my Dear Wife Pam' and 'Darling Pam'. The new Mrs Smith was understandably upset.

In court Smith was fined £25 for contracting a bigamous marriage. He promised to divorce his first wife and settle down with his second and he also arranged to have the offending tattoos removed. 'It'll be worth the £50 doctor's fees to make a clean start', he assured the press.

Head Over Heels

Newlyweds Kenneth and Donna Kiehn posed dutifully for a series of wedding photos. 'Just one more picture', implored the photographer, and he motioned the couple backwards. Kenneth and Donna moved as ordered, still holding hands and gazing steadfastly into each other's eyes, until they suddenly disappeared off the balcony on which they were standing and plunged some thirty feet down, vanishing into the murky depths of the ornamental fountain below. Donna's mother remarked afterwards: 'They'll have a long recovery period. They were still holding hands when rescuers pulled them out.'

Who's A Pretty Boy!

In 1976 John Levermore, a tall, dark and handsome American professor of English, generously volunteered himself as a prize in a raffle held to benefit his college's amateur theatre club. He said, 'I hope I'm won by a beautiful bird. I'm hers for twelve hours and I promise to do practically anything she fancies.' Levermore's wish was granted, in a way. He *was* won by a bird – the parrot whose owner had bought a raffle ticket in the hope that the professor would use his talents to teach Polly to speak.

Keeping Him in His Place

It is traditional for the press to harass potential Royal couples. It is equally traditional for those pursued to be as non-committal as possible. For instance, Princess Anne, a few days before her engagement to Captain Mark Phillips was announced in 1973, answered a posse of reporters who wanted to know what he was doing visiting Sandringham: 'There is no romance between us. He is here solely to exercise the horses.'

Chains of Love

Frank Summers-Thompson appeared all around the world as 'The Man Who Can Escape From Anything'. For twenty years he appeared twice nightly, leaping unshackled from ropes, chains, handcuffs and boxes. In 1959 he married his partner, 27-year-old June Clark, whom he regularly 'sawed in half' during the show. Four years later, serving a brief sentence for fraud and false pretences in the Isle of Sheppey Open Prison, Summers-Thompson walked out. On checking his record the police and his young wife discovered that there was in fact *another* Mrs Summers-Thompson. Given that no divorce proceedings had intervened, the couple were due to celebrate their fifteenth wedding anniversary that year. When he was eventually recaptured the escapologist was tossed back into jail, this time charged with bigamy.

To Tell the Truth

Pierre Trudeau, Prime Minister of Canada and husband of author and 'personality' Margaret, 1969: 'I do not like indiscreet women.'

The Politics of Joy

Minister John Profumo informed a credulous House of Commons: 'There was no impropriety whatsoever in my acquaintance with Miss [Christine] Keeler.'

The Labour Opposition, self-righteously wrathful, were not amused, but Prime Minister Harold Macmillan stated on July 13: 'I was determined that no British Government should be brought down by the action of two tarts.'

Lord Hailsham, the Chancellor, added: 'A great party is not to be brought down because of a squalid affair between a woman of easy virtue and a proven liar.'

By the end of the year Macmillan had gone, pleading ill-health. Sir Alex Douglas-Home took his place, and in the 1964 election Labour put an end to 'Thirteen Years of Tory Misrule'.

Too Much

Richard Burton, referring to rumours of marital strife between himself and his wife, Elizabeth Taylor, in 1974: 'Elizabeth and I have been through too much to watch our marriage go up in flames. There is too much love going for us ever to divorce.' They went on to do just that.

Business Before Pleasure

Private Eye's euphemistic 'Ugandan discussions' have a notable predecessor. When, in 1928, one Miss Irene Savidge was accused in court of misbehaving on a Hyde Park bench with top economist Sir Leo Money, Miss Savidge explained: 'We sat down for a while to discuss matters of industrial economics.' The case was dismissed.

Five year later Sir Leo appeared once more before the bench, this time convicted of kissing a perfect stranger, one Miss Ivy Ruxton, on a Southern Region train running between Dorking and Ewell. He was fined 50/-.

If At First You Don't Succeed . . .

Barbara Hutton, heiress to the $45 million Woolworth fortune, announced her second marriage, to European aristocrat Count Kurt Heinrich Haughwitz-Hardenberg-Reventlow, in 1933: 'I've found happiness. I know this is safe and true. I love my husband and he loves me.' Three years later Barbara and the Count separated, and their divorce was finalized in 1941. She paid $375,000 into a trust fund for him.

Barbara then declared: 'I will never marry again.' But evidently she couldn't resist the star of *Gunga Din. His Girl Friday* and *The Philadelphia Story* – movie star Cary Grant. Hollywood dubbed it 'the Cash and Cary Marriage'. 'It's sheer heaven', Barbara sighed. But three years later Barbara had divorced Cary. To the reporters who were waiting outside the court, the former Mrs Grant promised: 'I will never marry again. You cannot go on being a fool for ever.'

In December 1952 Barbara Hutton tied her *fifth* knot, with Dominican diplomat and archetypal playboy Porfirio Rubirosa. On their wedding day the New York papers splashed a picture of Rubirosa's ex-girlfriend, Zsa Zsa Gabor, proudly exhibiting the black eye she claimed the playboy had given her when she refused to marry him. Rubi, as the press knew him and on whom Harold Robbins' *Aventurers* hero was modelled), received a string of polo ponies and a twin-engined airplane from his bride. 'It makes me sad to think of all the silly things I've done', said Barbara. Zsa Zsa wished them 'all happiness. I'm so glad he got married, or I probably would never have been able to get rid of him.' She gave the marriage six months.

Zsa Zsa was three months out – the Hutton-Rubirosa marriage lasted only a dozen weeks. Snapped the bride: 'Don't call me Mrs Rubirosa!'

By November 1955 Barbara had found Mr Right at last (No. 6), German tennis star Baron Gottfried von Cramm. 'I ought to have married him eighteen years ago', she cooed, 'But at that time I was married.' She gave von Cramm a set of pearl studs for the wedding. The groom said: 'I've been trying to marry her since I met her.' Barbara assured the press: 'Life has been terribly lonely. But no more lonely nights for me. This is positively my final marriage.'

Refuting strong rumours that they scarcely saw each other, and that their marriage was doomed, the van Cramms hit back in 1958. Gottfried: 'Ridiculous! Only business commitments have kept us apart. Ours is the perfect marriage.' Barbara: 'I swear I have never been so happy and contented before.'

A year later Barbara Hutton and husband No. 6 were quietly divorced. She told the world: 'I'm free as the air – no strings. I'm in a no hurry to go through all that crazy routine again.'

Four years later Barbara Hutton observed: 'I've been terribly unlucky with husbands,' But in 1964 she married a Vietnamese prince, Doan Vinh de Champacak. 'He's a composite of all my previous husbands' best qualities without any of the bad qualities. I am in an ecstatic state of happiness.' After the spring wedding she said: 'It's my lucky number. This is my seventh husband. We were married at 7pm on April 7th. I have never been so happy in my life.'

In November 1966 Barbara left her last prince. According to a newspaper report, she also left a cheque for $1 million for him at the reception desk of the hotel in Morocco where they were staying at the time. The switchboard informed her husband of her departure and, after appraising the contents of the envelope she had left, he spent the rest of the day on the golf course. Barbara Hutton did not marry again.

. . . Try, Try Again?

Mickey Rooney, 'Andy Hardy' to millions of US movie-goers, in 1949 married for the third time, telling the newspapers: 'If I don't make this one last, there's something wrong with me.' In December 1950 the London *Star* reported: 'Mickey Rooney and his third wife have separated. Miss Vickers said she would have custody of their ten-month-old baby.' One week later the *Star* continued: 'The Rooney's make it up . . . Said Miss Vickers, who had cancelled her impending divorce proceedings, 'We thought it would be a shame to spoil baby's first Christmas.'

However, ten months later the London *Evening Standard* announced: 'Mrs Rooney No. 3 gets divorce . . . "I saw him only two nights a week".' That same year, according to *The People*: "Tell the girls I'm still in the running", said Mickey Rooney, commenting on Hollywood reports that the end of his third marriage means the end of his love life.'

In November 1952 Mickey eloped with bride No. 4, Elaine Melinken, a Hollywood model. Rooney told reporters: 'This one is for keeps. We're really in love.' In 1953 Mickey Rooney was named in the trial of Los Angeles' leading Madame. 'I guess I'm just an excitable guy', explained Mickey to the *Sunday Dispatch* as he announced his 'trial separation' from his wife Elaine in 1957. 'Elaine is a normal girl who wants to be normally happy. It's just me and my business. We're still very friendly.' In June 1958 Elaine Rooney filed for divorce and told the press: 'This has been brewing for a long time.' She alleged grievous mental distress, suffering and anguish. Rooney paid out £136,320 in alimony.

In 1959 Mickey Rooney married wife No. 5, Barbara Thomason, another beauty queen and the first of his wives to be shorter than his 5 feet 3 inches. He called their marriage 'the perfect end to an imperfect journey'.

In June 1962 Mickey filed for bankruptcy. He told the US Federal Court he had $480,914 in debts and only $500 in assets. He claimed at the hearing that fast living and multiple alimony had cost him $4 million.

In December 1962 *The People* launched a five-part series in which 'Mickey Rooney Tells the Lot' with this: 'It's going to be a happy Christmas. As my adoring fifth wife kisses my bald patch (just left of centre) and puts out my slippers. I know darn well it's going to be a happy Christmas. Say what's happened to Mickey Rooney? . . . The image has slipped. Where's the wild man of Hollywood, the woman-chaser, the bookmaker's delight, the taxman's headache? Where are those bottles, bottles, bottles? Good friends, bring yourselves up to date. Mickey Rooney, model of 1962, is a much mellowed, nicely rounded gent of forty-two, happily married (fifth time lucky) and proud paterfamilias to three cute little Roonies. Sure the taxman's still yapping at my heels with a bill for £178,000. Sure I've gone bankrupt, sure four broken marriages have left their scars, alimony scars, sure I've still got a hangover from the wild years of boozing and bedding, but what the hell!'

In 1965 Mickey Rooney commented: 'Had I been brighter, the ladies been gentler, the Scotch been weaker, had the gods been kinder, had the dice been hotter, this could have been a one-sentence story: Once upon a time I lived happily ever after.' In January 1966 Rooney filed a divorce against his fifth wife.

In September of the same year Mickey married his sixth wife in a Las Vegas ceremony. Said Rooney: 'It's unimportant how many times a person is married. We don't think in chronological numbers. Margie's my wife and we're sure this is a good one.'

Three months later Margie Rooney sought a divorce 'on the grounds of mental cruelty', also alleging that her husband 'hid and secreted his assets'.

In 1969 Rooney made it seven: this wife was his press agent. In April 1972 Mickey announced that he had found Christ and lost any enthusiasm for Hollywood. 'I am my own man for the first time.' In October 1974 Carolyn Rooney filed for divorce.

A year later *The Sun* reported: 'Jan the eighth – she's next on Mickey Rooney's wedding calendar . . . Veteran film star Mickey Rooney, the eternal romantic, has found the girl of his dreams, again. "At last I've found the real one", he said, looking up into the eyes of 25-year-old singer Jan Chamberlain.'

'His previous wives just didn't understand him', said Jan. 'I'll be so different for him; understanding is so very important.' Although Rooney himself conceded that his other seven wives had understood him all too well, this time, he hoped, 'Love can conquer anything.'

EATING THEIR WORDS

Humble pie is never the tastiest of dishes, though it may be one of the most frequently consumed. And for those of us who manage to resist swallowing our own helping, it's always fun to watch others get it down.

Black Eye

In 1947 a very angry Eric Johnston, President of Hollywood's Association of Motion Picture Producers, told reporters, 'As long as I live I will never be a party to anything as un-American as a blacklist, and any statement purporting to quote me as agreeing to a blacklist is a libel upon me as a good American.' That same year his association released a statement which read, 'We will not knowing employ a Communist or a member of any party or group which advocates the overthrow of the Government of the United States by force or by any illegal or unconstitutional methods.

A Classic Case

'Too slow', 'confusing and irritating', 'too long', and 'issues too clear-cut and old fashioned' were some of the comments appended by thirteen publishing houses to Frank Herbert's science fiction manuscript *Dune*. The fourteenth published it , and *Dune* went on to sell ten million copies.

Powering On

Oliver W. Powers said, May 1960, replying to Kruschev's charge that his U-2 pilot son Gary was a spy: 'I don't believe any such words. He's not a spy.'

Creepy Crawfie

The *Sunday Express*'s Court reporter Louis Wulff was full of admiration for Miss Marion Crawford, the royal nanny. In an article in December 1946 headlined 'Training a Princess for the Throne', he gushed: ' "Crawfie", as she quickly became known in Royal Family Circles, was an ideal choice. Quiet, reserved in manner, with a far-ranging intelligence, she combined the qualities of firmness with an affectionate charm. Now that the Princess is a grown young woman Crawfie remains one of her closest confidantes and advisers, but no one outside the Royal circle *ever* hears Crawfie talk about her Royal charge.'

Two years later, Crawfie wrote a book called *The Little Princesses* in which she told all. Thereafter she was referred to in the press as 'Creepie Crawfie'.

Beached

Harold Wilson, leader of Her Majesty's Opposition, 1961: 'I myself have always deprecated – perhaps rightly, perhaps wrongly – in crisis after crisis, appeals to the Dunkirk spirit as an answer to our problems.'

Harold Wilson, Prime Minister, 1964: 'I believe that the spirit of Dunkirk will once again carry us through to success.

Cannon Fodder

Arthur Wellesley's mother was so disgusted by her son's slow academic progress that she withdrew him from Eton in order to save money for his younger brother's education. Put to work as a barrister, he was caught fiddling. Finally, in despair, his exasperated mother forced him into a military career, dismissing her wayward son as 'fit food for powder'. She meant cannon powder.

Her views may have changed when young Arthur, by then the Duke of Wellington, defeated Napoleon at Waterloo.

In Cold Print

In 1965 American author Truman Capote unleashed a bestseller titled *In Cold Blood*, in which a true-life murder was re-created using the techniques of a novelist. Although the public loved it, some literary purists were uneasy about the fictional gloss given to a factual event. Sniffed Capote's fellow author Norman Mailer, 'a failure of the imagination . . .'

In 1979 Mailer unleashed a bestseller titled *The Executioner's Song*, in which a true-life execution was re-created using the techniques of a novelist. The inside blurb read: 'A model of complete, precise and accurate reporting. *The Executioner's Song*, by the artist's profoundest intention and achievement, is a novel . . . The ancient art of storytelling. . .'

High Priest

Timothy Leary, the High Priest of LSD, prophesied in 1965: 'The United States will collapse by 1980.'

When asked fifteen years later why it hadn't, Leary retorted: 'My dear, what is time? You're talking to the person who brought you the 1960s!'

Burned Baby

Another 1960s saviour was American Black Panther leader Eldridge Cleaver, who in 1968 informed the readers of the *Saturday Evening Post* that the only thing to do with the White House was to 'Burn the mother down!'

But by 1980 Eldridge had modified his position somewhat, telling his readers: 'The greatest revolutionary statement in the world is ''Love thine enemy''.'

Never Trust Anyone Over Thirty

But the 1960s guru to whom Middle America would have been least inclined to offer up its daughters was Jerry Rubin, bearded, wild-eyed leader of the Yippies. 'Spread ideas that undercut the content world of America!' he harangued readers of his book *Do It*!. 'We must alienate middle class

Amerikkka . . . All watches and clocks will be destroyed, barbers will go to rehabilitation camps where they will grow their hair long.' Rubin's masterstroke was in 1967 when he stormed the New York Stock Exchange. Tossing dollar bills down onto the startled stockbrokers, he shouted from a balcony: 'We're here creating with our brothers and sisters in this revolutionary socialist movement!'

In 1980, after a career in health foods and fringe religion, a tidily clipped Mr Rubin started a new job as a $36,000-a-year securities analyst for the Wall Street firm of John Muir & Co. Declared the former scourge of the rich: 'Money and financial interest will capture the passion of the 1980s. Let's make capitalism work for everybody.'

Overtaxing Exile

In 1967, wealthy British industrialist Sir Bernard Docker set off with his wife for a life of bliss as a tax exile on Jersey. Explained Sir Bernard: 'There are lots of reasons for the move. Income tax is only 4/- in the pound and there are no death duties. We shall of course have our yacht *Shemara* down there. Jersey will be a very good base from which to go cruising.'

Less than two years later, Lady Docker announced that they were selling *Shemara*, pulling up stakes and heading off into the sunset. The trouble was their fellow tax exiles, as Lady D. explained: 'They're the most frightfully boring, dreadful people that have ever been born.'

Any Minute Now

Despite – or perhaps because of – her tireless battle against death and disease in the Crimea, Florence Nightingale was one of history's greatest hypochondriacs. In 1857, the year after she returned from the Crimea, she took to her bed convinced that her 'life hung by a thread' which could 'snap at any moment''. It eventually did – in 1910, when she was 90 years old.

What A Goer!

In 1968 motor racing ace Jackie Stewart gladdened the hearts of Britain's women's liberationists by declaring: 'I've never seen driving as a sexual thing.' The next year the same Jackie Stewart said: 'You treat a car like a woman. If you relate it to a woman – because it is a very highly strung and nervous piece of equipment – you can have this love affair with it. You have got to be able to understand it and comprehend its feelings and habits. You have to coax it sometimes to get the best out of it, you have to correct it and treat it gently, and at times, maybe on a different circuit, you have to give it a really good thrashing, because that is the only way it understands.'

Queen For A Day

New Statesman, August 16, 1968, page 200: 'There can be no rational explanation for this sudden attack of reginaphilia, a disease that has become increasingly rare in Fleet Street and is now almost entirely confined to the giddier pops.'

New Statesman, August 16, 1968, page 190: 'Next week, profile of the Queen. Paul Johnson.'

No Fooling

When the young Orson Welles announced his plan to broadcast over the radio a dramatization of H. G. Wells's *War of the Worlds* the day before Halloween, 1938, most of his colleagues in the Mercury Theatre dismissed the idea. 'Too fantastic', they sniffed. 'It just isn't believable.'

Welles, undeterred, pressed on with the plan. The night of the broadcast saw unprecedented panic throughout northeastern America as innocent listeners, believing the broadcast true, headed for the hills to avoid what one man, who rushed into a police station babbling, described as 'the terrible people spraying liquid gas all over the Jersey Meadows'.

Foot & Mouth Disease

Former American Vice President Spiro T. Agnew, began his career as Richard Nixon's running mate with this promise: 'I have often been accused of putting my foot in my mouth, but

I will never put my hand in your pockets.'

In 1973 Mr Agnew left office in disgrace. In his televized resignation speech he confessed: 'The intricate tangle of criminal charges levelled against me . . . boils down to the accusation that I permitted my fund-raising activities and my contract-dispensing activities to overlap in an unethical and an unlawful manner. Perhaps, judged by the new, post-Watergate political morality, I did . . .'

Queen for Three Days

Rumours began to circulate that Miss World of 1973, Marjorie Wallace, was being pressed to relinquish her title by the contest organizers, allegedly shocked by her personal conduct. Snapped a heated Miss Wallace to reporters who confronted her with the stories: 'I have no intention of renouncing my title. Is that understood? Got that? Good!' Three days later she called another press conference to announce: 'I am giving up my title.'

Queen for Seven Days

Marjorie's successor, Helen Morgan, though more staid in her nocturnal activities, fared just as badly. When it was discovered that she was in fact an unmarried mum, Miss Morgan, in the space of one week, went from 'I am honoured and excited to have won the title' to 'I have no intention of resigning' to 'I am resigning. I regret having entered the contest.' Her final comment was: 'I regret my decision to resign.'

Doctored Death

In 1975, while speaking in the American House of Representatives, Bill Young launched into a vigorous defence of the B-52 bomber. 'The B-52 has been an effective war machine. It's killed a lot of people.' Unfortunately this went down badly with a number of his constituents, who came away with the distinct impression that their Bill was something of a warmonger who approved of killing lots of people. So Bill had the *Congressional Record* altered to read, 'The B-52 has been an effective war machine which unfortunately has killed a lot of people.'

Doctor at Large

When announcing Dr R. H. Hales as the new $35,000-a-year Senior Medical Advisor at Whitehill, Indiana's largest state penitentiary, Mrs Waram Fulger, the Appointment Board's Chairman, gushed: 'Dr Hales gave a brilliant interview.'

Dr Hales retained his new position until his picture appeared in the local newspaper. Then it was revealed that he was in fact a 53-year-old inmate of Byeways, Indiana's largest lunatic asylum, who had escaped two days before his appointment by concealing himself in a disused icebox.

Indecent Proposition

In 1978 American tax reformer Howard Jarvis introduced to the voters his Proposition 13, designed to halve Californian property taxes at a stroke. One of its most implacable foes was State Governor Jerry Brown, who spoke out against it at every opportunity, declaring : 'Proposition 13 will replace one monster with another.'

The night Proposition 13 was passed by the voters – by a margin of almost two to one – Governor Brown made yet another speech on the measure. This time, he said: 'Proposition 13 creates challenges, it creates problems, but it creates an opportunity to make government in California a model for people all over the country . . . a great opportunity!'

Democratic Amounts

In 1921, after a short term as legal counsel to America's Firestone Tyre Company, 29-year-old Wendell Wilkie decided to branch out on his own. In saying goodbye, the formidable Harvey Firestone shook the young man's hand and confessed: 'I like you, young man, but I don't think you will ever amount to a great deal. I understand you are a Democrat, and no Democrat can ever amount to much.' Nineteen years later, Wilkie ran for President.

Curse of the Mimi

February 2, 1981: 'Aunt Mimi Lashes Ghouls!' screamed the headline. The story was that John Lennon's Aunt Mimi, who had raised the singer as a lad, was disgusted by the heartless entrepreneurs who were 'jumping on the bandwagon' and exploiting his death. What particularly riled Aunt Mimi was the sharp operator who was peddling copies of Lennon's birth certificate.

On February 6, 1981, the *Daily Star* ran a television advertisement breathlessly promising: 'For the first time, Aunt Mimi tells all! Even his wives don't know the full story . . . only the woman who raised him as a boy! Read it tomorrow in the *Daily Star*.'

Fear and Loathing

In 1976 Hunter S. Thompson, king of the Gonzo Journalists, wrote in *Rolling Stone*, after first explaining how a reference to Bob Dylan in a speech by then Georgia Governor Jimmy Carter intrigued him: 'At the moment, failing any new evidence that would cause me to change my mind, I would rather see Jimmy Carter in the White House than anyone else we are likely to be given a chance to vote for . . .'

In 1977 Thompson reneged, admitting to his readers that his endorsement of Carter was: 'the ugliest thing I've ever put into print. Carter is one of the three meanest men I've ever met.

THAT'S ENTERTAINMENT?

'A man is a critic when he cannot be an artist, in the same way as a man becomes an informer when he cannot be a soldier.' (Gustave Flaubert, 1846). Or, he who can, does, and he who can't, knocks him.

Classic Blunders

Tchaikovsky wrote, in his diary entry for October 9, 1886: 'I played over the music of that scoundrel Brahms. What a giftless bastard! It annoys me that this self-inflated mediocrity is hailed as a genius. Why, in comparison with him, Raff is a genius.'

After witnessing the first performance of the *Marriage of Figaro*, the Emperor Ferdinand's considered opinion was: 'Far too noisy, my dear Mozart, far too many notes . . .'

According to John Hunt, *not* one of the greatest 19th-century critics: 'Rembrandt is not to be compared in the painting of character with our extraordinarily gifted English artist, Mr Rippingille.'

Philip Hale, a Boston music critic, pronounced judgment in 1837: 'If Beethoven's 7th Symphony is not by some means abridged, it will soon fall into disuse.'

Connoisseurs of the beaux arts in *Blackwood's Magazine* in 1818 could have seen Mr J. G. Lockhart's review of a new poet, one John Keats, by profession an apothecary, who had offered the public *Endymion*: 'It is a better thing to be a starved apothecary than a starved poet. So back to the shop, Mr John. Back to plaster, pills and ointment boxes.'

Take Your Time

Time Out, April 30, 1976, page 36: '*The Chelsea Girls* (X) (Andy Warhol, 1966, US) . . . Unfortunately this is considerably more boring than its reputation (and Warhol's best work) would suggest.'

Time Out, April 30, 1976, page 42: '*Chelsea Girls* (X) (Andy Warhol, 1966, US) . . . One of the great ''classics'' of underground cinema that contains some of the most personal and startling sequences ever recorded. An intense documentation of superstar life at the notorious Chelsea Hotel.'

Ten-Ton Tosca

When the star of the Athens Opera Company's production of *Tosca* fell ill at opening night, it gave her talented (but, at 200 pounds grossly overweight) young understudy her first big break. Pacing nervously behind the scenes moments before the curtain was due to go up, the poor girl overheard a stagehand shriek derisively: 'That elephant can never be Tosca!' Enraged, the young soprano leapt on the offender, tore off his shirt and bloodied his nose. Then, with one bruised eye already beginning to swell, she stormed onstage and laid them in the aisles. Her name was Maria Callas.

Silent Running

'Who the hell wants to hear actors talk?' demanded Hollywood's famous studio boss H. M. Warner. Who indeed.

The British film director Anthony Asquith, speaking in 1929, commented, 'The talking film seems to me to be false and a hybrid.' (Asquith went on to make his name with such talkies as *The Winslow Boy* and, possibly the most wordy movie ever made, *The Importance of Being Earnest.*)

Film critic Ernest Betts: 'Personally, I am convinced that films should be seen and not heard . . . The imagination cannot work any longer, there is no mystery for it to work on.'

But the last word on the dreaded talkies can be left to *Punch*'s acerbic A. P. Herbert: 'They are doomed to an early and expensive death.'

Critic's Corner

When the talkies finally did arrive, they smashed as many careers as they created. Director Howard Hughes was half-way through shooting his aircraft epic *Hell's Angels* when sound made his leading lady – the Norwegian-accented Greta Nissen – unusable. Panic stricken, Hughes turned over his Metropolitan Studios to a huge talent hunt. One of the hopefuls to emerge was an 18-year-old blonde by the name of Harlean Carpenter. Unfortunately for Miss Carpenter, all did not go well with her screen test. Screenwriter Joseph March took one look at her and exclaimed, 'My God she's got a shape like a dustpan!' Howard Hughes shared this view: 'In my opinion, she's nix.' This might have torpedoed Miss Carpenter's career, but she survived – and later changed her name to Jean Harlow.

Howard Hughes was consistently unfortunate when it came to talent-spotting. He vetoed his director Lewis Milestone's choice for one of the male leads in *The Front Page*. Sneered Hughes: 'a little runt'. Milestone had wanted an unknown named James Cagney.

As a result of Hughes's thumb's down, *The Front Page* also lost out on another newcomer. Hughes dismissed Clark Gable with the line: 'His ears make him look like a taxi-cab with both doors open.'

Hughes was not alone in his myopia. The head instructor at New York's prestigious John Murray Anderson Drama School once told a youthful red-headed actress: 'Try another profession. Any other.' Luckily for her, Lucille Ball kept plugging and eventually became Hollywood's richest female star.

The scouting report for Fred Astaire's first Hollywood audition would have broken the spirit of any less dedicated hoofer: 'Can't act, can't sing, slightly bald. Can dance a little.'

When a studio worker was sent to greet the young Bette Davis on her arrival in Hollywood, he returned empty-handed, complaining that 'No-one faintly like an actress got off the train.'

Wind Blown

The film which caused the most red faces around Hollywood was, ironically, its greatest success – *Gone with the Wind*. In fact, it seems almost an accident that it was ever made at all.

MGM was among the first to come to grief. On being offered film rights to the novel, producer Irving Thalberg advised his boss, Louis B. Mayer: 'Louis, forget it. No Civil War picture ever made a nickel.' Said Mayer: 'Irving knows what's right.'

Next in line was 20th Century-Fox. Screenwriter Nunnally Johnson remembered, 'Long ago at 20th Century-Fox I was reading one of the innumerable synopses that were distributed each week and I paused when I came to the name of the hero: Rhett Butler. Undiscouraged, I pressed on. But when I came to the name of the heroine, Scarlett O'Hara, I dropped the whole matter. I had no intention of getting mixed up in another version of Terry and the Pirates and the Dragon Lady and Lace. What fools they were to think they could hoodwink me with rot like that!'

Later, when Jack Warner tried to tempt Bette Davis into playing the part of Scarlett, Bette took one look at the script and snorted: 'I bet it's a pip!'

Finally David O. Selznick wound up making the film – and his fortune. But even to the end there were still doubters. When Selznick offered the film's director, Victor Fleming, a percentage of the profits as part of his fee, Fleming snapped: 'Don't be a damn fool, David. This picture is going to be one of the biggest white elephants of all time!'

Bitching

In 1954, director Howard Hawks was considering a 21-year-old novice named Ivy Nicholson to play opposite Jack Hawkins in his multi-million dollar epic, *Land of the Pharoahs*. Ivy's screen test instructions read: 'You're quarrelling, and he slaps you. Just react naturally, as you would if you really got slapped.' The cameras rolled, Jack faked a slap, and Ivy, suitably roused, let out a bloodcurdling yell and buried her teeth in her leading man's arm. The test was suspended and Ivy sent home with the words, 'You're not quite up to the part.' Later she was replaced by Joan Collins.

Miss Collins's own fledgling steps in the movies were less than dignified. She began her career as a prostitute in *Turn the Key Softly*, became pregnant in *The Good Die Young* and revealed as much as could be revealed in the early 1950s in *The Decameron* but after *Cosh Boy* had been banned in Birmingham, Joan had had enough. 'I'm sick of being a movie floozie!' she wailed to the press. Of course, her finest moments were still before her – as the star of her sister's sex epics, *The Bitch* and *The Stud*.

Un-Loved

During the cut and thrust of 1920s Hollywood, MGM leading lady Bessie Love delivered what she no doubt thought was the *coup de grâce* to a rival. Chatting with studio boss Carmel Myers, she sweetly showed her claws with: 'I'll never forgive Joan for changing herself the way she's done. You know, she used to be so pretty, so pretty and kind of *round*, and her name, Lucille LeSueur, sounds so lovely.'

Myers obviously thought otherwise. As Bessie slowly faded out of the picture, he transformed the new svelte Joan Crawford into the industry's top pin-up.

Short-Term Stardom

Joan Crawford's mother, after her daughter had received an MGM contract offering a six-month try-out at $75 a week: 'Don't get carried away, dear. It says "six months".'

No Future

Mervyn LeRoy, after directing three unknown starlets in *Three on a Match*: 'I think Joan Blondell will be a big star, Ann Dvorak has definite possibilities, but I don't think Bette Davis will make it.'

Mathematical Wizardry

Actor Ed Wynn, turning down the part of the Wizard in the proposed film of *The Wizard of Oz*: 'The part's too small.'

Slow to Understand

An anonymous MGM producer, after the first viewing of *The Wizard of Oz*: 'That "rainbow" song is no good. It slows the picture down.'

You Got the Wrong Man

Film extra to Hollywood studio boss Adolph Zukor: 'Hey Shorty, got a match?'

Anonymous studio hand to director Mervyn LeRoy, who had made several successful films before the age of thirty: 'Hey, kid, where's the director?'

Your Money for My Wife

In May 1973 *Playboy* magazine's 'After Dark' section ran a snippet entitled 'Press releases we never finished reading', which reported: 'Negotiations have been completed by Warner Brothers for filmization of *The Boys in the Bank*, tentative title for the story of the much-publicized robbery of a New York bank last summer by a youth seeking to finance a sex-change operation for his boyfriend . . . ' In 1975 this became the box-office smash hit *Dog Day Afternoon*, starring Al Pacino.

Good Heavens!

'Why do they want to see the rushes?' shrugged director Michael Cimino when United Artists executives began pressing him over his 'masterpiece', *Heaven's Gate*. Why? Because *Heaven's Gate* was already $25 million over budget, several hours over length, and even then was destined to become the most expensive movie flop ever.

It's Only Rock 'n' Roll

Back in 1960 the BBC was hardly 'attuned to youth'. Banning the pop shows *Wham!*, *Oh Boy!* and *Dig This*, a spokesman declared: 'The teenage vogue for beat music and rock 'n' roll is over. Now the demand is for pop music shows of a broad family appeal.'

Mr Justice Harman had spotted the decline of pop even earlier. In 1957 singer Tommy Steele came before him during a contractual lawsuit. The judge removed his spectacles, peered over the bench, and asked rhetorically: 'How long can this Tommy Steele last? Five months?'

American band leader Mitch Miller, on the appearance of a new music style called rock 'n' roll: 'It's not music, it's a disease.'

Frank Sinatra, on the same phenomenon: 'Rock 'n' roll is phony and false and sung, written and played for the most part by cretinous goons.'

And the Secretary of the North Alabama White Citizens' Council: 'Rock 'n' roll is a means of pulling the white man down to the level of the Negro. It is part of a plot to undermine the morals of the youth of our nation.'

Elvis Who??

Elvis Presley's first notes were crooned to Memphis studio boss Sam Phillips. After auditioning the young singer, Phillips scribbled a note, 'Elvis Presley – good ballad singer', filed it and forgot it.

To Phillips's credit, he did eventually retrieve the note and set Elvis on his way. Others would have preferred shooting him. When asked if he would bid for the rising young star, Ed Sullivan, the kingmaker of American TV, croaked: 'Nothing in this great, free continent could make me put that boy on my programme.' Except, maybe, ratings. The following week Elvis was paid £17,000 to appear on Sullivan's show – the highest fee he had ever paid.

Jackie Gleason, the overweight comedian, informed the entertainment world in 1956: 'I tell you flatly, [Elvis] can't last.' The *Daily Mail*'s Jack Payne was of the same opinion: 'Singing in any form is foreign to Elvis.'

Even Elvis's own men were none too sure how long it would be before the bubble burst. Returning to Britain empty-handed after trying to sign Elvis to appear in the Café de Paris in 1956, Major Neville-Willing explained: 'He wanted £20,000 a week. They were very apologetic about asking such a high price, but Presley is going into the Army soon and he has to make his money quickly, they said. By the time he comes out, the rock-and-roll craze might be over.'

Which would no doubt have suited the *Manchester Guardian*'s D. W. Brogan, who wrote an article headlined 'Elvis and the Big Beat': 'Never has popular singable music been at a lower ebb than in this year of grace. Possibly in desperation, radio, juke boxes and sing-songs have fallen back on old classics like 'Daisy, Daisy'. The hits of 25 to 30 years ago, like 'Five-Foot-Two', are now ripe for revival. I attended more than one community sing and thought how superior in singability these old classics were to 'Heartbreak Hotel'. So at Avalon on Catalina Island we sang of Casey and his 'Strawberry Blonde', of Lucille and 'the Oldsmobile'. We sang 'Tea for Two', and, of course, 'Avalon', and in Boston, stronghold of the true, the beautiful and the archaic, they have revived 'Does your Mother Know You're Out, Cecilia?' Who will sing 'Blue Suede Shoes' ten years from now?'

Who wouldn't?

Bachelor Boy

England's answer to Elvis was Cliff Richard. In 1958 the *Daily Sketch* was asking its readers, 'Is this boy TV star too sexy?' When Cliff appeared on the BBC's *Oh Boy* show, a scandalized *Musical Express* spluttered: 'His violent hip-swinging during an obvious attempt to copy Elvis Presley was revolting. Hardly the kind of performance any parent could wish their child to witness. This is showbusiness – do YOU want it?'

But by the 1970s the popular press was fairly gobbling its own purple prose. For example, *The Sun* pronounced in January 1971: 'Cliff Richard is Britain's showbiz equivalent to the All-American Boy. He's as smooth as cream, relaxed as a garden hammock, and he's never been anything but very popular.'

But, unlike Elvis, Cliff had the unfortunate habit of expressing his opinions on subjects unconnected with the world of showbusiness. In 1963, after a tour of South Africa, he told reporters: 'This coloured thing, you don't really notice it at all; coloured servants out there don't really mind – they get their food and their board, so why should they mind? Gosh, you get coloured servants all over the world. They don't mind it at all.'

Cliff's Shadow

In 1961 Cliff's backing group, The Shadows, published an autobiography entitled *The Shadows, by Themselves*. In it, heart throb bass player Jet Harris listed his favourite drink as 'shandy'. But within two years alcohol had become a major problem.

But Roy Moseley, manager of Harris and drummer Tony Meehan, was confident that Jet's lapse was a passing phase: 'He fought all competition and won hands down. He has emerged the triumphant victor, having conquered fears, setbacks and possible pitfalls. Last year he won a nationwide music poll as best instrumentalist. This year – who knows? Maybe he and Tony Meehan together will emerge as the favourite instrumentalists of 1963. It could happen.' It could have, but it didn't. Some years later the press discovered Jet working as a bus conductor in Cheltenham.

Who!

On October 22, 1964, Kit Lambert, the fresh-faced manager of a Mod group called the High Numbers, received the following letter from John Burgess, the EMI executive in charge of hiring new talent: 'Dear Mr Lambert, I have listened again to the High Numbers' white labels, taken from our last session, and still cannot decide whether or not they have anything to offer. You may, of course, in the meantime have signed with another company, in which case I wish you all the luck in the world.' A dispirited Mr Lambert signed the group to the minor Brunswick label, where they all made a lot of money after changing their name to The Who.

Roll On!

Initially, the Rolling Stones had two managers. After watching their new acquisitions go through their paces, Eric Easton drew his partner, Andrew Oldham, aside and said: 'The singer will have to go; the BBC won't like him.'

Flop Tops

Brian Epstein first spotted The Beatles in November 1961, playing in a dank Liverpool basement called the Cavern. Said Brian, who ran a record shop: 'I want to manage those four boys. It wouldn't take me more than two half-days a week.'

That year Epstein went to London, touring the record companies. Among other rejections came the classic from Decca: 'Go back to Liverpool, Mr Epstein. Four-groups are out.'

Jay Livingstone, head of America's Capitol Records, on the eve of the first Beatles tour of the US: 'We don't think the Beatles will do anything in this market.'

Allan Williams, the Beatles' first manager, after falling out with John Lennon: 'You'll never work again!'

Comedian Arthur Askey once bumped into Paul McCartney backstage at a concert. Quipped Arthur: 'You'll never get anywhere with a daft name like that.'

Henry Mancini, darling of middle-of-the-road music: 'The Beatles will never last.'

Allen Klein, the manager who presided over the Beatles' break-up, always harboured hopes that the end was really only a new beginning. In 1970 he conjectured, 'You know what will happen at Wembley? George will announce that he's gonna do a concert, right? About two weeks later, Ringo will say, 'Hey, I'll play too!' Then John says he's gonna be there. Everyone will wanna know where Paul is. He'll think I'm trying to embarrass him. You betcha!'

Tiny Who?

Tiny Tim's parents were not exactly enthusiastic about his prospects as an aspiring young entertainer: 'I'm sorry to say, in all fairness, you'll never be anything. You'll never get anywhere singing in that sissy voice.'

Cher Delight

Photographer Richard Avedon told the dark and sultry pop star, Cher: 'You will never make the cover of *Vogue* because you don't have blonde hair or blue eyes.' When she did, *Vogue* sold more copies than at any time in its history.

The One that Got Away

On May 23, 1974, the *Bath and West Evening Chronicle* began an article with: 'Bandleaders come and go, but the perennial Duke Ellington, like Tennyson's brook, seems destined to go on forever.' The next day Duke Ellington died in a New York hospital.

Ulterior Motives

Sylvester L. 'Pat' Weaver, Vice-President of NBC-TV, in 1954: 'The grand design of television is to create an aristocracy of the people, a proletariat of privilege, the Athenian masses. To make the average man the uncommon man. TV will make adults out of children.'

Money Talks Dirty

Chas Jankel, songwriter and performer with Ian Dury's Blockheads, commented in 1979: 'I refused to write the music (for 'Plaistow Patricia') as I didn't really get off on the words. I thought any song that starts off 'Arseholes, bastards, fucking cunts and pricks' is not exactly going to be a major No. 1 world hit.'

The album *New Boots and Panties*, which featured 'Plaistow Patricia', remained in the top twenty for more than a year.

Self-Destruction

Atlantic Records' executive, John Kollodner, keen to sign up singer Peter Gabriel in the US, managed to manipulate a sneak preview of Gabriel's new LP. His verdict: 'Commercial suicide!' However, on its release the album went straight to No. 1 in the UK and into the US top fifty. Kollodner and Atlantic parted company soon after, and Kollodner went to Geffen Records. There one of his first signings was – Peter Gabriel.

High Flyer

Two months, before he died of an overdose in 1980, singer-songwriter and heroin addict Tim Hardin told *Wet* magazine: 'I can watch people die. I've seen people croak and I've thrown them out the window . . . out the window because you don't want the body in the pad. You might get busted anyway for what you're already doing.'

Monkey Business

Irish actor Peter O'Toole in *Playboy*, 1965: 'I think it's time there was an innovation to protect the author and the actors and the public from the vagaries of the director. Given a good play and a good team and a decent set, you could put a blue-arsed baboon in the stalls and get what is known as a production.'

In 1980 Mr O'Toole's production of *Macbeth* showed just why that play is considered cursed by theatre people. 'Baboon' was possibly the only critical epithet he did *not* incur.

THE GREAT DICTATORS

Power is the great aphrodisiac; it also seems to offer its possessors an unlimited opportunity for foisting their views on others. That such views veer between the self-aggrandizing, the hypocritical and the unappetizing has never, apparently, been considered a drawback.

The Red Menace

In 1886 a 16-year-old Russian boy named Vladimir Ilyich Ulyanov graduated from the Simbirsk Gymnasium school and applied to enter Kazan University. However, as young Vladimir's elder brother Alexander had recently been executed as a terrorist, his chances seemed remote until the Director of the Gymnasium, one Fyodor Kerensky, penned a personal letter of recommendation. Wrote Kerensky: 'Neither in nor out of school has a single instance been observed when Ulyanov by word or deed caused dissatisfaction to his teachers or the school authorities. Religion and discipline were the basis of [his] upbringing, whose fruits are apparent in Ulyanov's exemplary conduct.'

Vladimir won a place, whereupon he became a confirmed atheist, led a number of student riots, was arrested and finally expelled. Later he changed his name to Lenin and later still he overthrew the Provisional Government of Alexander Kerensky, the son of his old schoolmaster.

Few of his contemporaries foresaw Lenin's rise. In 1905 he led a group of dissident 'Marxists' in 'a campaign of mass agitation'. Sniffed Police Director Zvolianski: 'A small clique. Nothing will come of them for at least fifty years.'

When Lenin appeared in Russia after exile under the Czar, the Provisional Government was not unduly disturbed. Socialist Deputy Skobelev assured the Cabinet that Lenin was 'a has-been'. The influential writer Sukhanov decided that 'Lenin in his present state is so unacceptable to everybody that he represents absolutely no danger.' After Lenin's maiden speech before the Assembly, Foreign Minister Paul Miliukov could hardly contain his delight. 'Lenin completely failed', he beamed. 'From this he will never recover!'

It's Only Logical

According to Afghanistan's Moscow-supported President Amin, in October 1979: 'Since the leader of our Party is automatically the leader of the working class, our Government is supported by all the working people.'

Somoza's To Go

General Anastasio Somoza was never much for subtlety. When reporters once asked about the fact that his family seemed not only to own the greater part of Nicaragua but to have settled into the Presidential seat for ever, he scoffed: 'Dynasty, hell. We're a family that likes politics and know our job!' A year later yet another of his sons began his political ascent. Shrugged the General: 'You know how children are – they like to follow in their father's footsteps.'

But it was under fire that Somoza's true grasp of politics came to the fore. With the country in uproar, civil war raging, daily massacres, and dire food shortages, the General warned the rebel Sandinista forces: 'Please don't force me to apply the law because above all I love my citizens.' With that he proceeded to bomb the entire country to within a hundred yards' radius of his fortified concrete bunker. As the situation slid further into bloody chaos, the General peered out of a gun slit across the ruined city and said: 'I have no reason to abandon my constitutional post.' When the Americans withdrew their support he was gone within the week.

Break My Heart

In 1925 Hugh Walpole had his first meeting with a young man just out of prison and back on the run from the German police – Adolf Hitler. Wrote Walpole later: 'Tears poured down his cheeks. I thought him fearfully ill-educated and quite tenth-rate – pathetic. I felt rather maternal to him.'

Adolf—I Hardly Knew You

Bridget Hitler was an Irishwoman who married Adolf Hitler's elder brother Alois. According to Mrs Hitler's memoirs, the future Führer once visited his brother in Liverpool in 1912. Whatever abilities Bridget had, perception was certainly not amongst them. 'I found him only weak and spineless', she later wrote of her brother-in-law.

Uncle Adolf

Willie Hitler, Bridget's son and Adolf's nephew, was equally myopic. Visiting England in 1937, Willie, then twenty-six years old, declared: 'My uncle is a peaceful man. He thinks war is not worth the candle.'

Uncle Joe

Josef Stalin, to Hitler's Foreign Minister Ribbentrop: 'The Soviet Union is interested in having a strong Germany as a neighbour, and in the case of an armed show-down between Germany and the Western democracies, the interests of the Soviet Union and of Germany would run parallel to each other. The Soviet Union would never stand for Germany getting into a difficult position.' The most difficult position Germany managed to get herself into was her invasion of Russia soon after.

Marshal Josef Stalin's victory speech at the end of the Second World War, broadcast from Moscow at 8pm on May 9, 1945, began with these stirring words: 'Comrades! The great patriotic war has ended in our complete victory. The period of war in Europe is over. The period of peaceful development has begun.'

Nice As Can Be

Mr Dobi, president of the Yugoslav Smallholders' Party, following a meeting with Stalin in 1948: 'This great man of the Soviet peoples struck me as a wise, kindly old man. His eyes reflect peace and kindness, that is why the peoples he is leading are so attached to him.'

The Little Corporal

Adolf Hitler, 1933: 'I have never delivered a firebrand speech!

Adolf Hitler, 1924: 'Christ was the greatest early fighter in the battle against the world enemy, the Jews. The work that Christ started but could not finish, I – Adolf Hitler – will conclude.'

Adolf Hitler, 1934: 'We are winning international respect.'

Adolf Hitler, 1934: 'By this revolution the German form of life is definitely settled for the next thousand years.'

Idi-Otic

Were ever so many so enthusiastic over so little?

In January 1971 a Ugandan Army officer named Idi Amin toppled the left-leaning regime of Milton Obote and installed himself as the country's new leader. He did so, he said, reluctantly: 'Matters now prevailing in Uganda forced me to accept the task that has been given me by the men of the Ugandan Armed Forces on the understanding that mine will be a caretaker administration, pending an early return to civilian rule when free and fair elections will be held, given a stable security situation.'

So great was the British Foreign Office's relief at (so they thought) having seen the back of Milton Obote that even when, a week later, Amin declared himself Supreme Head of Uganda, nary a murmur was heard in opposition. In fact, the fulsome praise heaped on 'Big Dada' bordered on the embarrassing.

Under the headline 'Good Luck to General Amin', the *Daily Telegraph* enthused: 'General Amin, a beefy, softspoken man of the Madi tribe, sets an example of self-restraint . . . I wish him the best of British luck.'

The *Daily Express* had more of the same. Under the headline 'The Champ Who Rose From the Ranks to Seize Power', their journalist wittered: 'Military men are trained to act. Not for them the posturing of the Obotes or the Kaundas who prefer the glory of the international platform rather than the dull but necessary tasks of running a smooth administration. Amin looks capable of that task.'

The *Telegraph* countered with 'Good Riddance to Obote', and continued: 'First reports seem to suggest that [Obote's Government] is being replaced by a military government which, with any luck, may turn out to be of like nature and ambitions to those which have successfully brought law and order and relatively clean administration to Ghana and Nigeria.'

The *Guardian* called Amin's first press conference 'an exercise in magnanimity'. And after the great man had graced London with a visit, the *Daily Mirror* concluded: 'A thoroughly nice man. He looks every inch the heavyweight he once was. But in conversation he was as gentle as a lamb.'

The press was not alone, by any means. Britain's politicians were positively falling over themselves to offer bouquets. Tory MP Evelyn King, writing in the *Telegraph* under the headline 'General Amin, Uganda's Gentle Giant': 'Softly spoken but direct, General Amin is typical of independent Africa's newer and more realistic approach to world affairs.'

Nevertheless, the rise and rise of Idi Amin was still essentially a media event. A year after Amin's seizure of power, the *Financial Times* was calling the General 'without a doubt, a benevolent, honest, dedicated and hardworking man'.

The next day *The Times* went even further: 'One feels that Uganda cannot afford General Amin's warmhearted generosity.'

Amin also had supporters in Uganda itself. Officers in his old regiment called him 'a splendid chap'. John Akii-bua, a Ugandan athlete, said in 1972: 'It's a good land; a big garden, a cow and you can live.' Exactly for how long was another matter. By the end of 1972 it was conservatively estimated that Amin had murdered eighty to ninety thousand of his compatriots.

Still, Britain's press still went all the way with Idi. Judith Listowel, writing in *The Times* at the beginning of 1973: 'President Amin has the support of the Ugandan people who still believe he is bringing them real independence. He is admired by all Africans . . . not only does Idi Amin's luck still hold, but it is possible that this semi-literate peasant from the West Nile district can write a new chapter in East Africa's history.'

Spink's, the London medallists who designed some of the President's array of decorations, chided: 'People tend to laugh at the President over his decorations, but this is quite unwarranted. He is a valued customer who helps our exports.'

As late as 1975, when Dada addressed the UN, the *Evening Standard* headlined its story: 'Every Inch a Field Marshal!' By then the United States Ambassador was calling him a 'racist murderer'.

Inevitably, the euphoric outpourings of the press began to wane. Amin went on the offensive. 'Uganda has among the best prisons in the world and people from many countries are eager to visit them,' he boasted to the *Guardian* in January 1976. (Later it was alleged that prisoners in these famous prisons had been forced to execute each other with sledge hammers.)

The same day he told the *Telegraph*: 'As leader of Uganda I am known as Big Daddy President Amin Field Marshal. I am not a stooge of the imperialist, I am one of the strongest African leaders against any sort of imperialism, colonialism, apartheid, Zionism.'

Two days later he informed the *Mail*: 'Politics is like boxing – you try to knock out your opponents.'

In April 1979, Amin hit the canvas, and Tanzania delivered the knock-out punch. Big Dada was defiant – and ill-advised – to the last. At first he warned the invading Tanzanian army it was 'sitting on fire and would not survive'. That tactic having failed, he announced grandly: 'As Conqueror of the British Empire, I am prepared to die in defense of the motherland, Uganda.' With that he fled to Libya.

If only someone had heeded Walter Cootes, the last British Governor of Uganda, who in 1962 had cabled his superiors about Idi Amin: 'I warn you, this officer could cause you trouble in the future.'

The Black Shorts

Lord Rothermere's *Sunday Dispatch* was an avid supporter of law and order and all who stood for it, regardless of nationality. In November 1925 this leading article appeared: 'In no country will Signor Mussolini's escape from the assassin's hand be welcomed more cordially than in Great Britain, for nowhere else, outside his native land, has the Italian leader more numerous or more ardent admirers.'

The doughty lord was also much impressed by other rising martial movements. In 1934 he headlined another story: 'Hurrah for The Blackshirts!' Leading the Blackshirts at that time was a supremely confident Sir Oswald Mosley. In 1938 he boldly predicted: 'We shall reach the helm in five years.'

Proud as a Peacock

He had it all – wealth, power, his own Peacock Throne. How could the Shah go wrong? Who could have guessed? Certainly not *Weekend Magazine* in June 1967: 'No one can guess what it cost when the royal stork arrived in Teheran, capital of Persia, seven years ago. The Peacock Throne, symbol of 3,500 years of unbroken monarchy, was trembling as the nation awaited the birth of a baby . . . the baby *had* to be a boy . . . a 41-gun salute – it *was* a boy. Planes flew over the city dropping millions of rose petals as the crowds sang and danced in the streets. Within hours thousands of baskets of exotic flowers had formed a huge carpet around the royal palace. Four great arches around the palace were covered with more than a million carnations and chrysanthemums. The Shah declared a national holiday and a tax rebate for everybody. Lucky charms poured into the palace, as well as tons of sweetmeats. Scores of prisoners were freed and others had their sentences reduced. So the baby heir to unknown wealth and problems became Prince Reza and united a nation in rejoicing and loyalty to the throne.'

Certainly not British Airways' in-flight magazine *High Life* in September 1976: 'The sartorial world is indebted to the Shah for his tenacious acknowledgement of the grandeur of monarchy in an age when levelling down too often robs us of the grand spectacle which was once upon a time more commonplace . . . Conspicuous consumption in these democratic days reflects not an oppressive ruling class, but a basic national prosperity which is unaffected by the sumptuousness of the people's representative. It is a pleasure to see it.'

Definitely not Jimmy Carter, who told the Shah in 1977: 'Iran is an island of stability in one of the more troubled areas of the world. This is a great tribute to you, Your Majesty, and to your leadership and to the respect, admiration and love which your people give to you.'

Nor even Farah Pahlavi, the Shah's third wife, who answered questions about Savak, the Shah's murderous secret police, in 1978 with: 'You know, in Iran we have laws like everywhere else and if people break those laws they must go to jail . . . each system has its weaknesses, each has its positive aspects.'

And finally, not poor Reginald Davis, whose book *Royal Families of the World*, published by Collins in 1978, contained this unfortunate observation: 'On September 16, 1979, His Imperial Majesty Mohammad Reza Pahlavi Shahanshah Arayemeh, will have ruled Iran for 38 years, and in the 2,500 years of his country's monarchy no ruler has been held in greater respect and affection . . . restoring their country from social and economic backwardness to a state of dignity, prosperity and political stability, the people have bestowed upon him the title Arayemeh – Light of the Aryans. It was a token of deep affection and no title he holds is more dear than this.'

It's All a Matter of Semantics

Park Chung Hee, President of South Korea, in 1974: 'We have no political prisoners – only Communists and others involved in conspiracies against the country.'

Noms-De-Plume

In 1975 the new Marxist Government of North Yemen issued this decree: 'All official titles used in correspondence, addresses, mass media and in various quarters will be completely abolished, to be replaced by the "brother" at all levels.' The decree was signed by Lieut-Col Ibrahim Hamadi, Chairman of Command Council, Commander-in-Chief of the Armed Forces.

Diamonds Are a Boy's Best Friend

Former French President Giscard D'Estaing once warmly described Emperor Bokassa of the Central African Empire as 'France's best friend in Africa'. But that was before the Emperor massacred several hundred schoolchildren because they refused to buy their school uniforms from one of his relative's factories. Later, the exiled Bokassa seriously embarrassed his old friend by revealing that he had on more than one occasion given gifts of diamonds to the French President and his family.

TOO MANY CROOKS

Crime may well pay, but sometimes there's a pay-off the villain doesn't appreciate.

Fly Boys

In January 1981, at the Annual Fly-Swatting Championships held at a pub in Eaglehawk, near Bendigo, Australia, a sheepshearer called 'Spot-On' Mick stole the honours. He out-swatted seven other finalists, racking up a new world record of 148 points. Mick wiped out rivals 'Peabeu' Pete and 'Ian the Exterminator' when a Queensland greenfly, worth a hefty 20 points, fell before his deadly swatter. Waving aside admirers, Mick modestly explained, 'I got lucky.' This was over-modest and also untrue, for later that day the judges disqualified four of the finalists, including Mick himself, when it was discovered that 'some of them had extra help. They had bits of meat in their pockets.'

Heavy Mob

A taxi drew up outside a scrap-metal merchant in Dundee's Milnbank Road. A man alighted and withdrew from its boot a large and weighty sack. He then entered the premises, approached the first man he saw and inquired 'Is it OK – there's no police about?' Unfortunatley he had chosen a plain-clothes policeman, who had been making a routine visit to the shop, and the man was arrested.

Daylight Robbery (1)

The managers of a bank in Nashville, Tennesee, arranged for its tellers to watch an educational film entitled 'Tips on How to React to a Holdup'. As they gazed at the screen, two masked robbers entered the under-staffed bank and stole $12,979 from the under-protected tills.

Pizza Excess

In 1944 the American forces stormed into Sicily, driving out the occupying Germans and starting a push upwards through Italy. Captain Charles Dunn found a most useful interpreter who doubled as an informer against those corrupt Sicilians who were operating a lucrative black market. Dunn was so impressed that he gave the man a handwritten recommendation to certify that he had 'been employed by me as my personal interpreter since January 28, 1944. He has been invaluable to me, is absolutely honest, and as a matter of fact, exposed several cases of bribery and black-market operations among so-called trusted civil personnel. He has a keen mind, knows Italians as do few people, and is devoted to his adopted home, the USA, and all American Army personnel'.

However, Army Intelligence later discovered that Captain Dunn's obliging interpreter, with 'Lucky' Luciano and Meyer Lansky, had dominated US organized crime for a decade before vanishing back to his native Italy, bare steps ahead of the law. Vito Genovese was eventually extradited back to the US where he was finally jailed in 1958.

Armed and Unready

Mohammed Razaq, a Wandsworth grocer, was standing peacefully behind his counter in July 1979, when a young man came into his shop and demanded: 'Give me the money in the till or I will shoot you.' A puzzled Mr Razaq pointed out that the young man had no gun, whereupon he replied that unless the money was forthcoming he would *get* a gun – and then shoot him. Shortly after this exchange, he left the shop.

A Dog's Life

'Hand over the takings!' demanded the man waving a revolver in the main South Coast branch of a London bank. As the terrified teller moved to comply, the gunman tripped over Bosco (the manager's dog), fell across a desk and was stunned by a blow from the teller's cushion. He was later sentenced to life imprisonment.

The Kiss-Off

After he had finished robbing her home, the burglar bent over his 81-year-old victim, gave her a kiss, and said, 'You were always kind to me.' Whereupon the retired Cleveland school mistress recognized the intruder as her favourite pupil of 1925, Fergus Wayne. On her positive identification, Fergus was subsequently charged with robbery.

Takes One to Know One

American showman extraordinaire P. T. Barnum is perhaps best remembered for his oft-quoted dictum: 'There's a sucker born every minute.' What is less well remembered is that in 1855 Barnum invested over half a million dollars in a swindle called the Jerome Clock Company. The loss bankrupted him.

Kray-Zee

Mrs Violet Kray, interviewed about her son, East End 'businessman' Ronald Kray: 'I used to hear things about my Ronnie, but I have learned by now never to trust what other people say. I knew him, others didn't.'

The 'others' who didn't know Ronnie must have included Frank 'The Mad Axeman' Mitchell. In 1966, while serving a stretch, Ronnie and the Axeman became friendly. When the Axeman was charged soon after with the attempted murder of a fellow prisoner, Ronnie intimidated the eye-witnesses, briefed an attractive female barrister to defend him, and even had a suit made so the Axeman could look his best in the dock. Said a grateful Frank of Ronnie and his twin, Reggie: 'the two best friends a man could hope for'. Later, the twins sprang their friend from prison. However, Frank became a nuisance, so on the pretext of spiriting him away to a mansion in the country, Ronnie and Reggie allegedly lured him into a waiting van and pumped him full of lead.

Cooked Book

On December 7, 1971, Vice-President Albert R. Leventhal of New York's McGraw-Hill Publishers announced a major coup: his firm's acquisition of 'the world publishing rights to a 230,000-word transcript of the taped reminiscences of Howard Hughes'. This was very impressive, since no one had seen the reclusive multi-millionaire in over a decade. Sceptics murmured of fraud and forgery, but McGraw-Hill soon put paid to that with a press release, apparently prepared by Hughes himself. 'I believe', it read, 'that more lies have been printed and told about me than about any living man. Therefore it was my purpose to write a book which would set the record straight.' Donald M. Wilson, another McGraw-Hill executive, stated, 'We are absolutely certain of the authenticity of this autobiography and we wouldn't put McGraw-Hill's and *Life* magazine's name behind it if we weren't.' The company then began paying Hughes's go-between, author Clifford Irving, instalments of the $750,000 they were advancing on the book.

However on March 13, 1972, Clifford Irving, his wife Edith and associate Richard Susskind pleaded guilty in New York to criminal charges, specifically an attempt to defraud McGraw-Hill of $750,000. The real Hughes gave a telephone interview, and the Irvings were jailed.

Feel the Width

In Spring 1964 washing machine magnate and czar of the Rolls Razor empire John Bloom was riding high. 'I'm an idea man', he told *Newsweek* magazine. 'I sling my ideas out to my staff and say make them work. I look for things where the trading systems are fuddy-duddy, archaic, then I move in.

Home-movie equipment, we're going to start in April. It'll be easy. The TV rental business – more than 50 per cent of the TV sets in Britain are rented. There shouldn't be any problem making money here. And think of the business when colour comes in.'

Around the same time Bloom launched 500 million trading stamps, rejoicing in the name 'Supa Golden'. Mr Frank Lewis, head of stamp distribution, told the press: 'Of course we're not pushing the John Bloom image, but we believe that Mr Bloom's head on each stamp is a personal guarantee of security to the housewife.'

But by the end of the summer Bloom's hopes were in ruins. His home-movie scheme collapsed when every projector proved faulty; he never began his TV rental plans; the bottom fell out of the cut-price washing machine business, and Bloom was finished. The Rolls Razor empire had fallen by August 1964 with £4 million worth of debts and Bloom himself was indicted with obtaining money under false pretences.

Penny Lane

'I have the ability to think like a thief', declared wheeler-dealer Beatles manager Allen Klein to the rock music paper *Melody Maker* in 1972. But Klein, who had already fallen out with former clients the Rolling Stones, found that in 1973 his contract with John, George and Ringo (Paul had long since sought advice elsewhere) was not renewed. The US tax authorities, on the other hand, continued to pursue his more intimate acquaintance, and in 1979 he was sentenced to two months in jail for income tax violation.

Blunt Instruments

'I am a Comintern agent', announced Foreign Office good-time boy Guy Burgess to a friend in 1938. Nothing happened. Thirteen years later, Burgess waved farewell to a sailor on

Southampton docks. 'Back on Monday', he lied. With him was fellow Comintern agent Donald Maclean, who had introduced Burgess to his wife Melinda just the night before as 'Roger Stiles'. Maclean had then vanished, explaining that 'Mr Stiles and I have to keep a pressing engagement. I don't expect I'll be back very late, but I'll take an overnight bag just in case.' Neither man ever returned to Britain.

Four years later, as Intelligence interrogators, the press and the Commons searched for proof of a 'third man' and cited H.A.R. 'Kim' Philby as the prime suspect, Prime Minister Harold Macmillan stated unequivocally: 'I have no reason to conclude that Mr Philby has at any time betrayed the interests of this country, or to identify him with the so-called 'third man', if indeed there was one.' Six years later Philby announced his rank as a KGB colonel as he defected to Russia.

Slip-Up

In 1974, pursued and, in the case of the *Daily Express*, preceded by a clamouring media, Chief Superintendant Jack Slipper of Scotland Yard landed in Brazil to capture the elusive Great Train Robber Ronald Biggs. Meeting Biggs, he told him, 'You're under arrest. I'm taking you back to London on the next flight out of Rio.' But Slipper was wrong. Biggs fought extradition, Slipper went home in disgrace, and the train robber went on to avoid extradition again, this time from Barbados, seven years later.

Fag-End

A prominent 72-year-old Philadelphia businessman, who combined legitimate trading with running a massive inter-state cigarette smuggling ring, believed firmly that however hot things became, a bribe would always see him OK. In February 1980 he boasted to North Carolina supplier: 'As soon as they started feeling around here, yeah, we got the guys. What he didn't realize was that his supplier, too, was one of 'them' – an FBI informer, wired up with a tape recorder. The incriminatory tapes proved the old man's undoing. He was charged, with the informer and eight accomplices, with smuggling more than four million cartons of cigarettes, thereby defrauding Pennsylvania state tax authorities of $7.5 million over seven years.

Fine Fun

Emil Savundra, the genius behind Fire, Auto & Marine Insurance, one of the major financial swindles of the 1960s, appeared in February 1967 on David Frost's TV show. He seemed unperturbed by Frost's allegations of fraud, and when asked by his interrogator why he took so blasé a view of his crime, he replied 'But of course, it was all fun'. Later that week the fun was over: Savundra was arrested and at his trial was fined £50,000 and jailed for eight years.

Earlier that year, after numerous compaints against Fire, Auto & Marine, the Board of Trade had made an investigation. They declared, 'On the evidence available, there appears to be no immediate danger of insolvency.' Only one week later Fire, Auto & Marine applied to go into liquidation, leaving hundreds of thousands of customers uninsured.

Daylight Robbery (2)

In August 1975 a customer in a Philadelphia bank pushed a note across to the teller. He murmured, 'I am a bank robber. Give me the money.' But before the teller was able to respond, the next man in the queue pushed a gun into the robber's ribs. 'I am a policeman', he announced, 'and you are under arrest.'

Come and Get Me

On May 17, 1974, the members of the revolutionary Symbionese Liberation Army were holed up in a Los Angeles suburb, facing a force of 300 police and FBI marksmen. The media were out in force. Donald DeFreeze, known as 'Cinque' the SLA leader, told them: 'I know I am going to die, and all of my people know they are going to die, but we are going to take a lot of pigs with us.' In the ensuing shoot-out, telecast coast-to-coast, the SLA duly perished, but not one policeman was harmed.

Tea for Two

The two solicitors of Hay on Wye, Major Henry Armstrong and Mr Oswald Martin, sat down for a convivial tea in the spring of 1921. Major Armstrong passed Mr Martin a scone ('Scuse fingers') Mr Martin ate it, chatted and eventually left. Later that night he fell violently ill with acute stomach ache. Although he recovered, Mr Martin was unhappy and justifiably so. The scone, it transpired, was dosed with arsenic, the same arsenic with which the Major had recently poisoned his wife Katherine. Henry Armstrong was hanged at Gloucester Jail on June 30, 1922.

Unholier than Thou

In September 1979 curate Nicolaos Stavrakis lashed his parishioners in the magazine distributed by St Andrew's Church, Caerphilly. Upbraiding them for gambling, smoking and fornication, Stavrakis declared: 'Having mentioned it before, I assume people prefer to ignore what I say. As I have said before, I love you all whether you are made up or not. If the wearing of lipstick is that important to some people, they will have to come to church without it . . .'

But while he spread the Word in the pubs and clubs of Cardiff's dockland, after closing time the saviour became a sinner himself, searching the streets for girls who would accept the lifts he offered. These, sometimes led to secluded hillsides and violence, and in February 1981 'the Sex Fiend Curate' (*The Sun*) was jailed for 12 years for three savage rapes.

Lonely Hearts

Three hundred Parisiennes answered the following advertisement in French 'Lonely Hearts' columns between 1915 and 1919: 'Single gentleman, aged 45, £400 a year, desires to marry homely lady of similar age and income.' Unfortunately, the chosen seven had pledged themselves to Henri Landru, 'the French Bluebeard', who, one by one, took their money and killed them, later disposing of their corpses. From the scaffold in 1922 Landru claimed, 'It is not the first time that an innocent man has been condemned', but the guillotine fell nonetheless.

Cock (Up) of the North

'By planning you can drink life to the full'. Thus read the thoughts of T. Dan Smith, Newcastle entrepreneur, as headlined in the local press, when, 'a practical visionary', he was entrusted with the chairmanship of the Northern Economic Planning Council by Prime Minister Harold Wilson. He promised to make Newcastle 'the Brasilia of the North East', but in January 1970 Newcastle's go-ahead darling seemed to have come unstuck and he was charged with corruption. The case foundered, though, and in his 1971 autobiography Smith could boast 'I have found myself exposed to accusations of graft and corruption . . . I can vouch for the fact that during all my time on Newcastle City Council and later at the NEPC there has been no cleaner administration in Britain. Getting things done is not synonymous with pulling a fast one.' Newcastle's boosters breathed again.

Until, that is, July 1972, when John Poulson, an architect, claimed at his own bankruptcy hearing that he had given Dan Smith £150,000 over eight years. 'What for?' he was asked. 'I can't think', replied the hapless Poulson. 'He never produced anything. He used to tell me he was doing this and that and the other.' Smith, who had recently told the collected architects of the RIBA how 'disgusted' he was 'at the way contracting firms approached and entertained councillors on a scale that almost approached corruption', was tried in 1974 for these and other malpractices. Evidently he had been in the practice of bribing councillors to give contracts to his public relations firm, Dan Smith PR. He had also promised Poulson lucrative work that had never materialized. Smith was jailed for six years in 1974.

The Mackintosh Man

Sir Joseph, later Lord Kagan, commented in August 1974 following the publication of a Green Paper on the Wealth Tax: 'If you ask me if I enjoy being taxed, the answer, of course, is no. But if the wealth tax is going to be used to ease income tax at higher levels, then it must be a good thing for the future of the country and of my children. I hope that the tax will change the pattern so that merit and hard work are rewarded at the expense of merely having.'

In 1980 Lord Kagan was jailed for a number of offences, including tax fraud.

On the Beach

Hansard for May 7, 1974, reports a question from the Right Honourable Member for Walsall North, John Stonehouse, to the Secretary of State for the Home Office, 'whether he will review the arrangements for preventing drowning accidents.'

Roy Jenkins, then Home Secretary, replied that a working party was being set up to examine this problem. The committee, however, did not extend to Miami, Florida, where, sometime later, the same Right Hon John Stonehouse went for a swim, remarking, 'I think I'll have a quick dip before dinner.' He then deposited a pile of clothes on the beach and vanished, presumed by family, press and public alike to have drowned either deliberately or by accident. He was not discovered until he was mistaken in Australia, for the missing Lord Lucan.

Gold Thrush

The great Wilson Mizner, conman extraordinaire and hustler sans pareil, won additional fame by singing to the otherwise cultureless miners in Nome, Alaska's 1890s goldrush capital. Apparently the hard-bitten diggers felt Mizner's voice was operatic. At the peak of his success, warbling the hits at a New Year's Eve get-together, Mizner delighted the local bigwig, 'Diamond' Jim Wilson, proprietor of the Anvil Saloon and head of the Nome Fire Department. Jim Wilson raised his glass and asked the assembly to drink 'to Wilson Mizner, the best damned songbird in Alaska'. Alas for Diamond Jim, the glass had barely reached his lips before he dropped dead of apoplexy. Mizner, never one to pass up a chance, slipped out of the now chaotic party, went straight to Wilson's safe and cracked it.

Daylight Robbery (3)

It was business as usual at Pedigo's Grocery in Dallas, Texas, one afternoon in 1974. A man approached the check-out till, put a couple of items on the counter and said, 'Let me go and see what Momma wants.' 'Sure, son', said the clerk. Moments later the customer returned, brandishing a gun. 'Momma says to clean out the register,' he ordered. The clerk obeyed and the gunman left with $400, accompanied by an elderly lady.

Someone has Blundered

Mrs Bessie Gilmore, when told that her son Gary was being held for the murder of two people in Utah, replied: 'Well, there has to be a mistake. No matter what else, he is not a killer.'

Shopped

In 1972 a man walked into a California bank, thrust a water pistol in the cashier's face and handed over a note which read: 'Milk, loaf of bread, pick up laundry'. When the puzzled cashier pointed out the mistake, the would-be bandit panicked and fled. He was caught outside the bank when his car failed to start.

Wire Less

In 1913 an inventor called Lee de Forest was brought before the courts and charged with fraud for selling stock in his Radio Telephone Company. According to the District Attorney at the trial, 'De Forest has said in many newspapers and over his signature that it would be possible to transmit the human voice across the Atlantic before many years. Based on these absurd and deliberately misleading statements, the misguided public has been persuaded to purchase stocks in his company.' De Forest later became one of the leading pioneers of early radio.

WAR IN OUR TIME

'History is littered with wars that no one believed would happen.' (Enoch Powell) That's never stopped anyone waging them.

Forget the Alamo!

In 1836, forces led by the Mexican General Santa Anna surrounded a small force of Texans in the fort of Alamo in what would eventually become the state of Texas. The American commander, W. Barret Travis, sent out a last message through the Mexican lines. 'I am besieged by a thousand or more of the Mexicans under Santa Anna. I have sustained a continuous bombardment for twenty-four hours and have not lost a man. The enemy have demanded a surrender . . . I have answered the summons with a cannon shot and our flag still waves proudly from the walls.'

Within the hour Travis and the other 181 defenders had all died at the hands of the victorious Mexicans.

Civil Defence

General Sedgwick, Union general during the American Civil War, peered over a parapet at the Battle of Spotsylvania in 1864. His last words were, 'They couldn't hit an elephant at this dist . . . '

Poetic Licence

Matthew Arnold, the 19th-century British poet, opined at the outset of the Franco-Prussian War: 'You can be sure of the

French always beating any number of Germans who come into the field against them. They will never be beaten by any nation but the English, for to every other nation they are, in efficiency and intelligence, decidedly superior.'

War of the World

H. G. Wells, writing in 1914 on 'The War That Will End War': 'This, the greatest of all wars, is not just another war. It is the last war.'

Even so, rumours were rife when the Secret Service intercepted a telegram stating 'One hundred thousand Russians now on way from Aberdeen to London'. Visions of tramping Cossacks eventually gave way to relief, however. The communication referred to a shipment of eggs.

Earl Haig, Commander in Chief of Britain's forces in the Great War: 'Bullets have little stopping power against the horse.'

In July 1914 Arthur Conan Doyle abandoned Sherlock Holmes to pen a story on unrestricted submarine warfare, but Admiral Penrose Fitzgerald made the official attitude clear: 'I do not myself think that any civilized nation will torpedo unarmed and defenceless merchant ships.'

Within a year German U-boats had sunk the *Lusitania*, and 1198 people went down with her. Shortly before the disaster her captain, William Turner, had reassured his jittery passengers: 'On entering the war zone tomorrow, we shall be securely in the care of the Royal Navy.'

Curiouser and Curiouser

In 1919 the *Daily Herald*'s political cartoonist, Will Dyson, pictured the signatories of the Versailles Treaty as they left Paris. Clemenceau was turning to his companions and remarking, 'Curious, I seem to hear a child weeping.'

In the background was a sketch of a child, and beneath the infant was the legend 'Class of 1940'.

Six years later the French delegate to 'the final peace settlement', the Locarno Pact of 1925, M.Aristide Briant, welcomed the principle of German equality: 'We are Europeans. Away with rifles, machine guns, cannon!'

In February of that year Adolf Hitler refounded the Nazi Party.

Peace in Our Time

The *Daily Express* May 23, 1938: 'Britain will not be involved in war. There will be no major war in Europe this year or next year. The Germans will not seize Czechoslovakia. So go about your own business with confidence in the the future and fear not.'

The *Daily Express* September 30, 1938 announced, in a seven-column banner headline: 'The *Daily Express* Declares That Britain Will Not Be Involved In A European War This Year Or Next Year Either'.

Neville Chamberlain, British Prime Minister, returned from a conference with Hitler at Munich in 1938 and announced: 'I believe it is peace for our time.' Or, as the Fuhrer is said to have remarked: 'He seemed such a kind old gentleman, I thought I'd give him my autograph.'

A Bit Sas

In 1939 a Dutch officer serving at the Netherlands Legation in Berlin, Major Gijsbert J.Sas, began getting tips that Hitler, turning away from Central Europe, would soon be invading Holland, Scandinavia and the West. But his government were sceptical and they rejected his information. And no Nazi invasions were launched. Sas checked with his informant – apparently the delay was purely due to adverse weather.

In spring 1940 Sas contacted his bosses again. There was definitely going to be an attack this time, on Denmark and Norway. The Dutch pooh-poohed him, the Danish refused to listen and the Norwegian diplomat contacted was himself pro-Nazi and simply squashed the information. Copenhagen's Foreign Minister read Sas's message and snorted 'Nonsense!'

Days later both Denmark and Norway were overrun by Nazi troops. Weather again curtailed further invasion plans, and once more the Dutch ignored a desperate Sas. On May 9 he telephoned the Hague: 'It's tomorrow at dawn.' Indeed it was, but the Dutch Government were adamant: Sas was crying wolf. When the Germans did march in, the Dutch hadn't even bothered to destroy the vital bridges across the Meuse.

Call Me Meyer

Reichsmarshall Hermann Goering, head of the Luftwaffe, 1939: 'No enemy bomber can reach the Ruhr. If one reaches the Ruhr, my name is not Goering. You can call me Meyer.'

His Master's Voice

At 11 pm on the night of May 10, 1941, a searchlight unit near Glasgow spotted a Messerschmitt 110 pass above them, then circle before plunging towards the ground while a parachutist floated gently down nearby. The man was Rudolf Hess, once Hitler's deputy, now desperate to negotiate peace with England. Interrogated by an RAF intelligence officer, Hess declared: 'I have a very important message for the Duke of Hamilton', citing a friend he had met at the Berlin Olympics five years earlier.

Back in Germany Hitler declared Hess insane, and in England he was given no serious hearing. Imprisoned during the war, he was jailed in Berlin's Spandau Prison after the peace. He remains there to this day, since 1967, the solitary inmate of a block of 600 cells.

Dead Reckoning

On October 2, 1942, the gigantic transatlantic liner, the *Queen Mary* temporarily sailing as a troopship, ploughed through the Irish Sea crammed with 10,000 US servicemen. She was protected from the long-range German bombers, who threatened shipping on this last leg of the crossing, by the cruiser HMS *Curacoa*. To avoid the undersea threat of submarines, the *Queen Mary* pursued a zig-zag course, changing direction continually. The slower cruiser took up position five miles ahead, but within a few hours the liner had caught up. As the ships drew level and the *Queen Mary* started another zig-zag, her Captain, Cyril Illingworth, told his helmsman, 'Don't worry about the cruiser, she'll keep out of the way. These chaps are used to escorting. They won't inter-fere.' With that, the *Queen Mary* sliced the *Curacao* in half.

Haw De Combat

Jean Herold-Paquis, French Vichy Government propagandist, broadcast the daily news throughout the war concluding each bulletin: 'Like Carthage, England will be destroyed.'

In Berlin, William Joyce ('Lord Haw Haw') likewise heral-ded the British defeat, promising in his book *Twilight over England*, published in English on German presses: 'When the smoke of battle has rolled away . . . I hope and believe that . . . the ordinary people of England know their soul again and seek in National Socialism to advance . . . with their brothers of German blood . . .'

Joyce was captured after the war and hanged as a traitor in Wandsworth Jail on January 3, 1946.

All-American War

Thirteen months prior to Pearl Harbour, Franklin Delano Roosevelt was campaigning in Boston on October 30, 1940:

'And while I am talking to you mothers and fathers, I give you one more assurance. I have said this before, but I say it again and again and again: your boys are not going to be sent into any foreign wars.'

Nip in the Air

In 1922, while war-weary Europeans were barely recovered from the Great War, America was thinking, just a little, of their Pacific possessions. They were not worried, however. On October 16 the US Secretary of the Navy welcomed the growth of worldwide radio communications, stating happily: 'Nobody now fears that a Japanese fleet could deal an unexpected blow on our Pacific possessions. Radio makes surprise impossible.'

Years later, in September 1941, this attitude persisted. The magazine *Aviation* declared, in a piece that painted the Japanese air force as accident-prone and utterly vulnerable to attack: 'America's aviation experts can say without hesitation that the chief military airplanes of Japan are either outdated already or are becoming outdated.'

On August 3 1941, Franklin Roosevelt had met Winston Churchill for the Atlantic Conference in Newfoundland. When the English leader mentioned the Japanese, FDR smiled and joked, 'I think I can baby them along for three months.'

He managed just four. On December 7, 1941, a strike force of 368 'outdated' Japanese fighters and bombers eviscerated the US Pacific fleet at Pearl Harbor, Hawaii. The Americans lost 19 ships and 3457 troops and civilians. The Japanese lost just 19 planes. Over the next few months before improved replacements arrived, the despised Japanese fighter, the Mitsubishi A6M2 Zero-Sen, wiped its American rival, the Brewster Buffalo, out of the eastern skies. Only one survived, captured intact and went back to Japan for testing.

The Pacific War effectively ended on August 6, 1945, when the first A-bomb demolished Hiroshima. But not everyone realized. Earlier that year Lieutenant Hiroo Onoda had been sent to Lubang, in the Philippines, to attack US air bases. His orders were explicit: 'You are absolutely forbidden to die by your own hand. It may take three years, it may take five, but whatever happens we will return for you. Until then, so long as you have one soldier, you are to continue to lead. You may have to live on coconuts. If that is the case, live on coconuts. Under no circumstances are you to give up your life voluntarily.'

It did not take three years, nor even five. Not until March 9, 1974, did Onoda, the sole survivor of his troops, emerge from the Philippine jungle. For thirty years, as one by one his troops died and search parties came in vain to winkle him out, Onoda had lived off the land, making guerilla raids as ordered on the islanders and killing perhaps thirty of them in all. Only when his former commanding officer, Major Yoshima Taniguchi, gave him specific orders to surrender, did Lieutenant Onoda come in from the cold.

Algerie Française!

The Second World War was barely over before the more compartmentalized wars, insurrections and struggles for liberation and the destruction of great Empires took up their various banners. Naturally, informed opinion knew best.

Wayland Young, Lord Kennet, writing in the *Scotsman* on August 21, 1954: 'The military insurrectionary nationalism which has swept Tunisia and Morocco does not affect Algeria at all. It is hard to see how any independence movement could make any headway here.' Two months later the Algerian War of Independence began.

Of course, the powers that be were blameless. Ian Todd, a journalist writing in the *Johannesburg Star* on September 25,

1956: 'Algeria under the French is a model of democratic rule, and the natives are a host of ferocious fanatics.'

Combat, the French Army's own magazine, waxed lyrical on Bastille Day 1957: 'The Paratroops, magnificent, strapping fellows, gay and affable. The Paras possess the prestige without which nothing is possible where Islam governs. Their audacity, their strength, their fighting virtue reassure the population. These boys, sons of our beautiful people, have found from the start the gestures, the attitudes that go to the heart of the ordinary people.'

This attitude was no doubt epitomized in the fate of a rebel soldier who was captured by some Paras, a story preserved in correspondent Herb Greer's *A Scattering of Dust* (1962): 'Every time he wouldn't answer, they cut off a little piece, starting with the fingers. They got half way to his elbow before he bled to death.'

The facts, perhaps, were summed up best by Lord Lambton, writing in the *Evening Standard* on January 23, 1958: 'The present troubles spring, in the main, not from French misrule, but from the efficiency of her health service, which has upset the balance of nature.'

Cuba Libre

Across the Atlantic, in Cuba, revolutionary forces under Fidel Castro were attempting to free their country from the dictatorship of President Fulgencio Batista, whose main governmental policies seemed to be suppression and the provision of a no-holds-barred haven for US organized crime.

The Times (December 4, 1956): 'General Batista, with little in the way of political tradition to support him, is leading his people painfully towards a broader based system. His is a benevolent despotism, and life in Cuba is more stable and more prosperous than at the beginning of his present lease of power . . . It is unlikely that the latest rebellion [by Castro] will shake his position.'

A day later, Alistair Cooke reported in the *Manchester Guardian*: 'It is reliably reported that as many as 150 men were gathered for the defence of Cuba and that the whole invasion force, all 40 of them, was wiped out . . . The invasion fleet, a yacht fitted out in Mexico, was badly damaged and might be unfit for charter for the rest of the season. Castro himself was certainly dead, and so was his brother.'

Castro persisted, miraculously resurrected, but Batista promised in July 1957: 'I have a pretty firm belief that the Castro problem will be solved in the best interests of the Cuban people.'

A year later, in October 1958, Major-General Fransisco Tabernilla, General-in-Chief of Cuba's Joint Armed Forces Command, grudgingly acknowledged 'a small group of saboteurs' whom he claimed 'refused to face up to military forces', but he assured the President that 'they are a wart which will be eliminated soon.'

On January 1, 1959, as Castro's men converged on Havana, Batista scavenged what he could and ran to exile. Later that year he remained the optimist. Speaking from Madeira, he announced: 'I give Castro a year. No longer.'

Thud and Blunder

The war in Vietnam which claimed so many lives, was also the pundits' graveyard. In two decades of hostilities politicians, generals and press all came badly unstuck time after time, always seeing light at the end of the tunnel when all there was was more tunnel. Indeed, the history of the whole sorry affair could almost be written in missed guesses. One of the few to see the writing on the wall was US General Douglas MacArthur, who opined back in 1950: 'Anyone who gets himself involved in a ground war in Indo-China needs his head examined.'

The first to lose their way were the French. During the early 1950s their skirmishes with the Communist Viet Minh slowly but inexorably escalated into full-fledged warfare. To General Henri Eugene Navarre, the future looked fine. Said the General in 1954: 'A year ago none of us could see victory. Now we see it clearly, like light at the end of the tunnel.' Six months later came the rout of Dien Bien Phu and the tunnel collapsed, burying 10,000 French troops. Exit France.

But the French were not alone in making rash statements. Flushed with their success, the Viet Minh began their march southward under the slogan: 'We will be masters of Saigon within six months.'

Enter America. As President John Fitzgerald Kennedy vowed on his Inauguration Day in January 1961: 'Let every nation know, whether it wishes us well or ill, that we shall pay any price, bear any burden, meet any hardship, support any friend, oppose any foe, to ensure the survival and the success of liberty.' It took thirteen years before America ate those words, but eat them it did.

At least the Americans started out on the right foot. When Under Secretary of State George Ball warned JFK soon after the Inauguration that if things kept escalating as they were, 'In five years' time we will have 300,000 men in the paddies and jungles of Vietnam', the President looked at him and said, shaking his head: 'Well, George, you're supposed to be one of the smartest guys in town, but you're just crazier than hell. That will never happen.'

The Bay of Pigs disaster in Cuba bolstered the President's early instincts not to get involved: 'One of the lessons I have drawn from this terrible experience is that we must have a political solution in Laos and not a military solution.

But, like the French before them, they couldn't resist. In 1962 the American Ambassador to Vietnam, Frederick Nolting, warned his Government of the incompatabilities of Americans and South Vietnamese. 'It's difficult, if not impossible, to put a Ford engine into a Vietnamese ox-cart', said Nolting. Replied Defense Secretary Robert McNamara: 'We can do it.'

Later that year McNamara made a trip to Vietnam himself. He was equally optimistic on his return. 'I found nothing but progress and hope for the future', he bubbled to the assembled press. Later, Vietnam would become known for a time as 'McNamara's War'.

America's man in Vietnam was President Ngo Dinh Diem, another incurable optimist. In October 1962 he said: 'Everywhere we are taking the initiative and we are doing this even during the rainy season, which heretofore the enemy has considered as favourable to him. Everywhere we are passing to the offensive, sowing insecurity in the Communists' reputedly impregnable strongholds, smashing their units one after another.'

Diem's arrival on the scene in 1960 was greeted with almost universal applause from his American allies: 'Doughty Little Diem!' crowed *Time*. 'One of Asia's ablest leaders!' said *Newsweek*. The American Government was even more fulsome. Vice President Lyndon Johnson dubbed Diem 'The

Winston Churchill of Asia'. President Kennedy himself coined the slogan 'Sink or swim with Ngo Dinh Diem'.

The South Vietnamese, however, had no intention of going anywhere near the water with Diem, a Catholic who by this time had begun massacring Buddhist priests. In 1962 he just missed death himself when rebel soldiers bombed his palace.

When JFK learned of Diem's narrow escape, he cabled this message: 'I am very gratified to learn that you are safe and unharmed, and wish to express my admiration for the calm and courageous manner in which you faced this destructive and vicious act'. Some months later Kennedy's CIA stage-managed the military coup which toppled Diem. After surrendering on an American guarantee of safe conduct out of the country, Diem and his brother were shot to death in an armoured car. The new government, hedging its bets, labelled the deaths 'accidental suicides'. Exit Diem.

Diem's successor was Major Nguyen Khanh. This time the Americans were convinced they had found the right puppet. Said Secretary of State Dean Rusk: 'General Khanh is on the right track: . . we've stabilized.' He said that on a Wednesday night. On the Friday another coup had ousted Khanh.

While the South Vietnamese politicians got on with the job of killing and toppling each other the American military got on with the job of winning the war. According to them it wasn't going to be much of a job. General Paul D. Harkins, US Commander in South Vietnam, spoke in Tokyo in October 1963: 'I can safely say that the end of the war is in sight.' General Charles J. Timmes, Commander of the US Military Assistance Advisory Group in South Vietnam (same date, same place): 'We have completed the job of training South Vietnam's armed forces.' Around the same time, one of General Harkins's aides was explaining to the *New York Herald Tribune*: 'What is mobility? Mobility means vehicles and aircraft. You have seen the way our Vietnamese units are armed – 50 radios, 30 or 40 vehicles, rockets and mortars and airplanes. The Vietcong have no vehicles and no airplanes. How can they be mobile?' How can they win?

Enter Lyndon Baines Johnson, 36th President of the United States. He began by talking tough: 'I'm not going to lose Vietnam. I am not going to be the President who saw South East Asia go the way China went.'

It sounded impressive, for a time. For example, Secretary of State Dean Rusk, in June 1964: 'Peace ought to be possible in South East Asia without any extension of the fighting. The next day the Government announced it was enlarging its force of advisors in South Vietnam by 5,000 (to a total of 21,000). Intoned LBJ: 'Our constant aim, our steadfast purpose, our undeviating policy is to do all that strengthens the hope of peace.'

LBJ, August 10, 1964: 'Our one desire – our one determination – is that the people of South East Asia be left in peace to work out their own destinies in their own way.' With that he signed the Tonkin Gulf Resolution, and for the first time Vietnam became a fully-fledged American war.

LBJ, this time during his October election campaign: 'We are not about to send American boys nine or ten thousand miles away from home to do what Asian boys ought to be doing for themselves.' LBJ won, and then all hell broke loose.

1965 was a year of unparalleled optimism for Ameria and her allies. Henry Cabot Lodge, the former Ambassador to South Vietnam, speaking to *Newsweek* in January, 1965: 'The military, economic, social and information programmes, together with the various technical programmes, have indeed built the springboard to victory.'

Secretary of State Dean Rusk, a few months later: 'There is little evidence that the Vietcong has any significant popular following in South Vietnam.'

And, of course, there was the man whose war it had become. Defense Secretary Robert McNamara. Early on in the year, when asked by an NBC television reporter whether Vietnam wasn't a bottomless pit, he replied: 'Every pit has a bottom.' After a visit to the beleaguered country he reported cheerfully: 'The major part of the US military task can be completed by the end of 1965.' And just to cap it: 'We have stopped losing the war in Vietnam.'

Speaking in Nebraska in June, LBJ promised: 'Peace is more within our reach than at any time in this century. Within six months he had raised the troop level from 150,000 to 475,000.

General Harkins had by now been replaced by General William Westmoreland. If anything, the new Commander in Chief was even more confident than his predecessor: 'We are making war in Vietnam to show that guerilla warfare does not pay.' He, too, suffered badly from tunnel vision: 'We can see the light at the end of the tunnel.'

It was not only the generals who were seeing lights before their eyes. Even America's allies got carried away on the rosy tide. Peter Samuel, an Australian pundit, writing in *The Bulletin*: 'The war is far from being over yet and the Vietcong may yet pull off a few spectacular feats, but the war is increasingly taking the form of a series of mopping-up exercises. These will be a bloody and horrible business, but there is no doubt that it can now be successfully accomplished.'

Arthur Calwell, the leader of the Australian Opposition: 'There is evidence to show that the Vietcong avoid Australians and on the whole do not want to fight us.'

In January 1967 rock guitarist Jimi Hendrix announced his own particular vision of the future: 'After China takes over the whole world, then the whole world will know why America's trying so hard in Vietnam.'

Hendrix went on to become a focal point for youthful protest, stopping shows with his version of the 'Star-Spangled Banner' replete with howling dive-bombers, bombs and machine guns.

According to LBJ: 'If we quit Vietnam, tomorrow we'll be fighting in Hawaii and next week we'll have to fight in San Francisco.'

And Dean Rusk: 'The other side is hurting and they are hurting badly.'

In 1967 General Westmoreland intoned: 'I have never been more encouraged in my four years in Vietnam.' Walt Rostow even went on record in *Look* magazine in December with: 'I see the light at the end of the tunnel.'

The next month the Vietcong launched their Tet Offensive, rocketing and mortaring seven supposedly 'safe' cities and sacking the US Embassy in the heart of Saigon. CBS News anchorman Walter Cronkite spoke for more than just himself when he asked helplessly, 'I thought we were winning this war?'

Exit LBJ and enter Richard Milhous Nixon. He began his run in the same fashion as his predecessors, with promises, promises. Accepting the Republican nomination in August 1968, he promised: 'My fellow Americans, the dark long night for America is about to end.'

However, when he finally reached the Oval Office he seemed to be reading from old speeches left behind by Lyndon Johnson: 'I am not going to be the first American President to lose a war.'

Admiral John S. McCain, the new Commander in Chief in the Pacific, spoke up in February 1969: 'We have the enemy licked now. He is beaten. We have the initiative in all areas. The enemy cannot achieve a military victory; he cannot even mount another offensive. Soon after, the Vietcong staged 159 raids simultaneously throughout the South, the largest number since Tet.

Undeterred, the Army plodded on. General Earle G. Wheeler, Chairman of the Joint Chiefs of Staff, in October: 'I judge that we are on the right track.' Perhaps it was the same track Australian Prime Minister John Gorton had in mind when he said to President Nixon: 'Sir, we'll go a-Waltzing Matilda with you.'

Secretary of Defense Melvin Laird broke the news of the new hope in October: 'President Nixon has a programme to end the war. That programme is Vietnamization.' He omitted to say whether the Vietnamese who would be carrying out the Vietnamization were to come from the South or the North.

By now it was not just Vietnam which was hitting the headlines. Secretary of State William P. Rogers reporting to the Senate Foreign Relations Committee in April 1970: 'It seems to us that our best policy is to avoid any act which appears to violate the neutrality of Cambodia.' The next month President Nixon invaded Cambodia with the words. 'This is not an invasion of Cambodia.'

In June President Nixon announced: 'The morale and self-confidence of the Army of South Vietnam is higher than ever before! The next month that same army announced that desertions had risen by 50 per cent.

General Earle Wheeler remained confident: 'If we just keep up the pressure, these little guys will crack.'

The year ended on what was meant to be an up-beat. On November 23, a US commando crew mounted a 'rescue raid' on a POW camp just 23 miles from Hanoi. Crowed Melvin Laird: 'We caught them completely by surprise.' This was no great achievement, since everybody there – soldiers, guards, POWs – had all left several weeks before.

Major Ted Sioong of the Australian Army speaking in 1971: 'The Vietnam war has been reduced to what we technicians call a police action.'

Colonel David Opfer, US Air Attache, berated reporters: 'You always write that it's bombing, bombing, bombing. It's not bombing, it's air support!'

When President Nixon finally signalled an 'end' to the war, he called it 'Peace with honour.' But in 1975 the Vietcong stormed down through the South to settle the matter once and for all. Some South Vietnamese, however, still swam against the tide. Colonel Luan, the Chief of the Saigon Police Force, who had gained widespread notoriety through his off-the-cuff execution of a Vietcong during the Tet Offensive, said to the American Ambassador: 'If you Americans think you're going to just walk away and leave us, you'll never make it to the airport. But they did, pushing their helicopters into the sea after them. The light they all kept seeing at the end of the tunnel had proved to be that of an express train.

SALE OF THE CENTURY

Never in the history of commerce have so many attempted to profit from the gullibility of even more.

Coco Loco

The Cocunut Grove was Boston's most fashionable nightclub in 1942, until one Saturday night in November. That night the place was packed, with a thousand guests – nearly twice the legally permitted limit – singing, dancing and dining. Among them was a party of twenty-five hosted by Hollywood's singing cowboy, 'Buck' Jones. Celebrating a successful 6,000-mile nationwide tour selling War Bonds, Jones drawled to newsmen: 'I'd like to relax tonight.'

By 10 pm the basement Melody Lounge, distinguished by its dimly lit decor of tropical foliage and plastic palms, was jammed full. One of the customers, dissatisfied with the already subdued lighting, decided to create an even cosier atmosphere by unscrewing a bulb from its coconut husk fitting. The manager assumed a bulb had popped and sent 16-year-old busboy Stanley Tomaszewski to replace it. Because the boy couldn't see properly he lit a match for extra light. The flame caught a plastic palm and within seconds the Melody Lounge was an inferno.

The customers collapsed in screaming, fighting panic. They surged towards the exit where a club bouncer, spreading his arms across the doorway, shouted: 'Nobody gets out of here without paying their bill!' Four hundred and ninety-two never got out at all.

Off the Track

In 1965 Wall Street thrilled at the proposed merger of two US railroad giants – New York Central and Pennsylvania Central. *Fortune Magazine* wrote: 'Few exercises exhilarate the financial world more than speculating what the Pennsylvania-New York Central Transportation company will be doing in ten years if the great plans now being laid for the system come to fruition.'

The merger went through simply enough, but the plans were less successful. In August 1970, five years later, Penn Central went broke to the tune of $4.6 billion – the largest bankruptcy in history.

On the Slate

The Times, 1969: 'Jim Slater has now earned himself a position of paramount respectability in the City for his novel and wide-ranging techniques.'

Slater, 1972: 'I want to become the world's greatest international financier in the next ten years.'

Patrick Hutber, writing in the *Sunday Telegraph* in 1975: 'Slater Walker is now safe from calamity.'

1975: Slater Walker collapsed.

999

In April 1970 Bruce Eckert, managing director of a London amusement arcade, travelled to Paris to check out a new and expensive fortune-telling computer. Asked if he would like a demonstration, he naturally said yes. The machine clicked, whirred and then spat out a seven-page document which advised him: 'If you are contemplating signing any contracts today, do not.'

'I laughed' said Eckert later. 'The future looked as if it would be in telephone numbers.' Back in London Eckert had the machine installed. There it took just five weeks, with overheads running at £200 a day and business almost non-existent, before the computer was crated up again. Admitted a rueful Eckert: 'We had a horrible failure.'

What's an Adverse Effect, Mummy?

The following advertisement ran in several British medical journals in 1960: 'Distival can be given with complete safety to pregnant women and nursing mothers without adverse effect on mother or child.'

Distival is also known by its more famous name of thalidomide.

It's Not What You've Got

Lord Roy Thomson, owner of the *Times* group, in 1961: 'I can tell you how to make money in newspapers – own them!' His son, who presided over *The Times* in 1980 when it was losing £2 million a month and eventually sold out to Rupert Murdoch, would not have agreed.

Typing Error

In 1968 a movement appeared in the UK called 'I'm Backing Britain'. This movement was shortlived but even in its heyday was better at producing mawkish copy than gross national product.

A good example is this *Daily Mirror* story, referring to five typists from Surbiton who worked an extra 30 minutes each day without pay as part of the campaign: 'It is possible that the five girl typists of Surbiton will, when the history of these confused times is written, become as famous as the six martyrs of Tolpuddle.'

The *Mirror* did not observe that the 'I'm Backing Britain' T-shirts with which the Government and eager entrepreneurs had flooded the country were quite clearly marked 'Made in Portugal'.

Flat as a Pancake

H. Ross Perot, a Texas millionaire, was wont to boast: 'I can spend money until the world goes flat.'

On one day his companies lost $200 million. Observed Perot: 'We had a bad day.'

Good Times Ahead

Leonard Macham, chairman of an international UK firm, assessed prospects for the 1970s in the *Times*, December 30, 1969: 'The 1970s, barring any major set-to between the major powers, show a steady increase in our national prosperity.'

Quaint

Mary Quant, fashion front-runner, in the *Daily Mirror*, February 6, 1970: 'We shall move towards exposure and body cosmetics and certainly pubic hair will become a fashion emphasis, if not necessarily blatant.' Ms Quant added that her own pubic hair had been shaved into a dainty heart-shape.

Mr H. L. Carter promptly complained to the Press Council: 'I do not think I have ever come across in any publication of any kind whatsoever such, filthy, lewd and disgusting material.' However, the Press Council disagreed.

Billion-Dollar Baby

In 1976 Montreal hosted the Olympic Games. As is customary, the authorities splashed out. They spent $50 million on a velodrome ($1 million per registered track cyclist in Canada); $1.5 million on walkie-talkie sets for security forces; $1 million on renting thirty-three cranes (more than the cost of buying them outright); and $500,000 on having the Montreal Symphony Orchestra mime to pre-recorded tapes. By the time the Games began – indeed even after they had finished – the main stadium and two special hotels were still being constructed. Yet Major Jean Drapeau, Montreal's first citizen, claimed blithely: 'The Olympic games can no more have a deficit than a man can have a baby.'

After the Games ended some 3700 tons of now useless material – from boxer's shoelaces to 10,000 TV sets – was put on the market at a fraction of its cost. The pricey debris filled warehouses the area of three soccer pitches and only the Canadian Army had sufficient trucks with which to move it all.

The hope had been that the Olympic facilities would then pay for themselves. Far from it. For instance, a mere 300 paying fans turned up to the first post-Olympic races at the Velodrome. The cost of maintaining the various stadia, building, etc, was estimated at $5.5 million a year and, the income at only $2 million. All in all the Montreal games came out with a very solid deficit: $1,000,000,000.

So Long As There's Life

In Africa, one of the leading brands of cigarettes is called 'Life'. During the 1950s, Kensitas cigarettes advertised themselves with: 'You get more out of life with a Kensitas.'

Sonny Money

Jack Nilon, Sony Liston's manager, assured reporters in 1963: 'Sonny's money is protected about as well as it could be legally protected.' After a promise like that it was only a matter of time before the unfortunate World Heavyweight Champion died broke and in debt in a run-down house in surburban Las Vegas.

Pinnochio

Jerry Perenchio, US boxing promoter, on the fight he arranged between Muhammad Ali and Joe Frazier in 1971: 'There's never been anything like it in my lifetime, very possibly since time began.'

Subsequent to the fight, however, Perenchio's business expertise came under fire – he was involved in some $58 million worth of lawsuits.

Is There Life After Death?

James R. Shepley, President of Time, Inc, in January 1970: 'You'd have to have a death wish to kill *Life* magazine.'

Gary Valk, Publisher of *Life*, 1971: 'We do not intend to go out of business; we do not foresee going out of business; and we have no contingency plans for going out of business.'

Life executive to prospective reporter, October 1972: 'You don't have to worry about *Life* magazine.'

December 1972: '*Life* magazine, in its weekly format, shuts down.'

You Can Say That Again

In 1970 the US National Society of Christians named as their 'Model City of the World' Belfast, Northern Ireland. The citation read: 'Belfast possesses a zealous Christian attitude and participates with an active interest in religious functions.'

Hard Sell

The US automotive industry is a fiercely competitive cutthroat arena, where every manufacturer searches for the perfect product. In 1954 the Ford Motor Company turned their attention to the middle range of consumers, hoping to cream off an important chunk of a market that bought seven million cars per year. They began developing an experimental car, 'The Edsel', named for Henry Ford II's father.

Top Madison Avenue advertising agency Foote, Cone & Belding were hired to launch the new model. Rather than boosting detail, size or capacity, all FCB offered the public were pictures of a gauzey shadow or a fabric-covered shape, but never the car itself. Some sixty copywriters put together 'the greatest advertising campaign ever conceived' (as Ford and FCB were proud to emphasize), aimed at the 'younger executive or the professional family on the way up'. Over a thousand brand new dealers were enlisted, 15,000 workers were put on the assembly-line and 800 Ford executives were seconded to the new model, all parroting the agency's slogan: 'Looks right! Built right! Prices right!'

Alas, by the time the launch came in 1957, the US economy had taken a downturn. Based on the previous statistics of boom, the Edsel was priced slightly high. That was its first mistake. Projected sales of 200,000 in the first year were never achieved; only around 100,000 were bought and the new dealers, each of whom had shelled out $100,000 for the privilege, shut their unprofitable shops.

If the price was wrong, so was the 'building'. The Edsel was plagued with every possible engineering foul-up. It didn't even look right. The grille, featuring the car's name in glistening aluminium, became a national joke. It was likened to a horse collar, an egg or a lavatory seat. Comedians gained surefire laughs just mentioning the dreaded name. The trade papers called it 'a mismanaged dilly'.

In 1958 Ford tried desperately to save the Edsel. A new campaign, costing $20 million was launched, and many of the early construction problems had been solved. But it was all too late. In November 1958 the Edsel was scrapped, and with it went an estimated $350 million of the Ford Motor Company's cash.

The Real Thing

In 1885 a drug manufacturer claimed: 'Cocaine can take the place of food, make the coward brave, the silent eloquent, free the victims of alcohol and opium habit from their bondage, and, as an anaesthetic, render the sufferer insensitive to pain.'

A year later, an early advertisement for Coca Cola proved that then, too, it 'added life', claiming: 'This Intellectual Beverage and Temperance Drink contains the valuable Tonic and nerve stimulant properties of the coca plant.'

Wonder Drug

When Thomas Sydenham perfected tincture of opium in 1670, he concluded: 'Among the remedies which it has pleased Almighty God to give to man to relieve his sufferings, none is so universal and so efficacious as opium.'

Grip of Steel

In 1933 two young cartoonists called Jerry Siegel and Joe Shuster, both aged just eighteen, invented a wonderful new character – an invincible man of steel whom they christened 'Superman'. For the next five years they hawked their creation. No one seemed interested, but in 1938 they hit paydirt in the shape of one Harry Donenfeld, a printer and magazine distributor, who had bought a bankrupt comic chain hoping to recoup some of the money its former owners had owed him.

Harry saw a specimen 'Superman' strip and decided to use it, although his staff at Detective Comics, Inc. were less than enthusiastic. Still, with a deadline to meet and two keen creators raring to go, Donenfeld decided to chance it. He offered Siegel and Shuster $10 a page and had them sign a release form. A letter explaining this form read: 'It is customary for all our contributors to release rights to us. This is the businesslike way of doing things.' They signed, thus losing the syndication, movie, radio and TV rights to their creation.

By 1940 Donenfeld was earning $100,000 a year from 'Superman'. When the unhappy creators complained and asked for a share in the windfall, the publisher simply threatened to replace them. Eventually he offered them a new contract, with a raise of $1000 per year between them, and sent them packing.

A real-life Superman might have helped, but he wasn't around. The disillusioned duo split up in 1948. Siegel was forced to ghost 'Superman' scripts for a meagre living, and Shuster went to live with his mother on Long Island. He never married, explaining: 'I never met a girl who matched up to Lois Lane.'

The King is Dead

In August 1966 flamboyant Cyril Lord, the Karpet King of Europe, predicted: 'In the long term I feel confident that with the increasing acceptance of tufted carpets we must go from strength to strength.' With that it was downhill all the way for Lord.

Numbered among his disastrous ventures were a Russian invention for making artificial astrakhan and the equipment and a factory for producing king-sized vinyl flooring, which never saw the light of day. A special computer-controlled storage system, designed in Norway, was found to be inapplicable to carpets. An English version of 'Astroturf', the fake grass, turned from green to blue in a matter of months and developed a 'slimy surface'. Instead of going from 'strength to strength', just two years later Cyril Lord Carpet Sale Limited went under.

Tommy's Gun

On January 31, 1922, readers of the New York *Herald* were faced with a full-page ad for 'the new one-man machine gun' invented by one John T. Thompson. Headlined 'A Sure Defence Against Organized Bandits And Criminals'. The ad claimed that 'The Thompson Anti-Bandit Gun is a powerful deterrent. It strikes terror into the heart of the most hardened and daring criminal. The moral effect of its known possession is an insurance of its own.' Among its many charms, continued the blurb, 'it can be carried under the coat for instant use.'

In the event, law enforcement officers were unimpressed, but 'hardened and daring criminals' loved Thompson's lethal brainchild. The 'Chicago typewriter' became the armoury hit of the era, underwriting the dubious exploits of Bonnie and Clyde, Al Capone, Ma Barker, the eponymous Machine Gun Kelly and the rest. It's finest hour, of course, was the St Valentine's Day Massacre on February 14, 1929.

Teeth and Smiles

In 1972 swimmer Mark Spitz came back to the US, garlanded with the record seven gold medals he had bagged at the Munich Olympics. Hollywood agent Norman Brokaw signed the champion up and announced: 'I call it the Mark Spitz Game Plan. My objective is to make an institutional tie-up for Mark very soon with two of the big blue-chip companies. It might be a GM or a Bristol-Myers, or somebody of that calibre. Then I'm planning to work out two TV specials in which Mark will star during the 1972-73 season. After that we're going heavily into the merchandising area worldwide. Then comes the personal appearance area. By the end of this year he will appear on two or three more shows . . . after this has been fully explored, we will approach the motion picture area, but not for at least six months. We feel that Mark Spitz will have a major motion picture career – I can see him playing the leading man in anything he does.'

Mark Spitz is now a dentist.

Snapped It

Hollywood director Mervyn LeRoy, to his assistant Howard Koch (later to become a successful Paramount producer): 'Howard, if you can get your hands on $10,000 put the whole bundle into a stock called Polaroid.'

Replied Koch with a dismissive shrug: 'Never heard of it.'

More Monkee Business

In 1966 came the Monkees. They were culled, in part at least, from an ad in *Variety* magazine which read 'Four insane, spirited and hip boys wanted, aged 17-21' and created, with a little help from a gullible public, by Don Kirshner of Columbia Pictures, a man who specialized, as his lawyer put it, in 'creative management'. The Monkees soon ran their course, leaving all concerned much richer.

Kirshner, on the other hand, who had parted company with Columbia (suing them for $35.5 million in the process), was still flexing his 'creative' muscle four years later. As a handout put it: 'It was the search for the Sound of the Seventies that brought producer Harry Saltzman and Don Kirshner together . . . the partnership of two of the world's most successful trend-setters began because Kirshner felt there was no genuine super-group around to launch the 1970s. Believing the time ripe for a star group, he approached the Canadian-born Harry Saltzman, the man who helped to create two of the super screen stars of the 1960s, the fictional James Bond and the factual Michael Caine.'

The band that Kirshner, scorning the likes of Crosby, Stills & Nash or Blind Faith, was preparing to foist on the new decade were called Toomorrow. 'Why the extra 'O'?' asked the dutiful media. 'Well', replied John Withers, of Licensed Merchandising Limited, whose clients already included James Bond and Noddy, 'you can't slap a licence on a word in general use. So we had to change the spelling.'

With that bridge crossed, the public were about to receive a flood of Toomorrow spinoffs – jewellery, sunglasses, clothing, shoes, sweets and cosmetics – all rejoicing in the then new concept 'Unisex'. On top of this there was a film called *Tomorrow* (one 'o'). Derek Coyte, of Eon Films, announced: 'There's no way of saying exactly how much money we've invested. Naturally it's a risk. But we wouldn't have put so much money into something we didn't think was going to be a success.'

The film, which featured the band being lifted to a desolate planet which they regenerated with their 'good vibrations', cost around $2.7 million. 'Every investment is a risk', admitted Coyte. 'Either the public buys it, or they don't. One must trust the experts.'

Not that the public were going to be let off the hook that easily, if off they wished to get. 'If they don't catch on as recording artists at first, they'll just go on making more records until it catches. If they haven't made a hit by the time the film comes out, I shall be disappointed. The substantial difference this group has over every other group is getting themselves involved with people who are established successes in showbiz like Kirshner and Saltzman.'

When cynics carped at a new Kirshner hype, Withers was quick to defend him. 'It's all quite different from the Monkees. They're not going to be built up as a group, but as four different characters. It'll be much easier to distinguish Toomorrow. For one thing, they all come from different parts of the world. And then, one's a girl and one's a black . . .'

Toomorrow bombed. The movie flopped; the record never sold; the flood of spinoffs piled up unappreciated. So much for Kirshner's hype. Or was it . . . that girl, what was her name? Olivia Newton-John, one time Australian child star, is with us still.

Born to Run

Riding precariously on the back of his brother Jimmy's then still popular presidency, Billy Carter set himself up in 1977 as proprietor of 'Billy's Beer', a brand that has supposedly helped Billy along with his own beer belly. Backed by the Falls City Brewing Company, the new brew hit the shops. Claimed its frontman: 'I could become the Colonel Sanders of beer.'

In the event Billy's Beer sank almost as fast as brother Jimmy's popularity. In less than a year the brewers and their beer had gone bust. The short-lived appeal of the stuff cannot have been helped by Billy's mother, Miss Lillian, who announced, 'I tried it once, but it gave me diarrhoea.'

Quick Change

In 1973 a New York City swimsuit corporation promoted their new season's costume, 'the trikini'. This seaside seducer, basically two pasties and a pair of panties, was 'a new concept designed to add new dimensions of poise. Most important, the cups cover bosoms fully and stay on in the water.' As eager press and buyers crowded round the poolside, a model dived in to demonstrate the trikini. When she emerged it appeared that the tri was now the mono . . . back to the drawing board.

Wage Slavery

A disgruntled Karl Marx, 1867: '*Capital* will not even pay for the cigars I smoked writing it.'

Conned

In 1977 Charles Frank Luce, the chairman of Consolidated Edison, New York's main energy suppliers, was asked how the old firm was holding up. He told the press: 'The Con Ed system is in the best shape in fifteen years and there's no problem about the summer.'

A matter of hours after this statement the whole city plunged into its worst electricity blackout in years.

Something Fishy

In 1976 Birds Eye, the frozen food manufacturers, put together a new sales campaign for one of their latest fish products. The treat: 'Cod Pieces'. It was surprising how far this campaign was allowed to proceed before someone noticed . . .

Psueds Live

'Top of the Pops' contender in 1967 was the 'Boston Sound', hailing from Boston, Massachusetts. Mort Nasatir, then head of MGM Records, puffed his Boston band Ultimate Spinach: 'Some of this music is so intellectual that it is a little like the poet T. S. Eliot with his seven layers of ambiguity in each line.'

Stranded

In 1959 a new advertising campaign hit the UK. It featured a cigarette called Strand. The copyline ran, 'You're never alone with a Strand', and the most notable TV spot featured a trench-coated figure lurking alone on a street corner, possibly – indeed probably – stood up by his date, lighting up a ciggie for solace. The campaign flopped utterly; the Strand brand never sold. The slogan, however, seems to have become engraved on the mass memory.

Ban the Gleam

Shortly after the first H-Bomb test in February 1954 this ad appeared in the pages of the *Pittsburgh Press*: 'The bomb's brilliant gleam reminds me of the brilliant shine Gleam gives to floors. It's a science marvel!'

Beanz Meanz Boobz

In 1972 advertising agency Young & Rubicam were about to launch their client Hunt-Wesson Foods' canned pork and beans in Canada. In England the product has been known as 'Big John's', and they wanted a Canadian equivalent. The basic translation for the French Canadian market – 'Grand Jean' – seemed insufficiently macho, so they changed it to the colloquial 'Gros Jos'. Development, packaging, design and the other necessities of the ad campaign went smoothly ahead and the launch was fixed. Then one French-speaking copywriter happened to read the label. It appeared, she pointed out, that the treasured colloquialism went a little far. 'Gros Jos' meant 'Big Tits'. The campaign was scrapped.

Beat the Crowds

The Government Tourist Bureau of South Vietnam ran this ad in the Malaysian press in 1965: 'Come to Vietnam. For Your Next Vacation. Something Different.'

Unhappy Landings

In a 1973 issue of *World Magazine* the following classified ad was placed: 'If you bought our course "How To Fly Solo in Six Easy Lessons" we apologize for any inconvenience caused by our failure to include the last chapter, entitled "How to Land Your Plane Safely". Send us your name and address and we will send you the last chapter posthaste. Requests by estates also honoured.'

All Fun and Games

Mayor Vladimir Bromislov, of Moscow, spoke in 1974 of the 1980 Olympic Games his town would be hosting: 'It will be open house – caviar, vodka, no problems about visas . . .'

Vote With Your Feet

In 1975 it was election time in Ecuador. Riding the media bandwagon were the firm of Pulvapies – manufacturers of a foot deodorant of that name. They conjured up a special campaign: 'Vote for any candidate. But if you want well-being and hygiene – Vote Pulvapies!'

On election eve they put out a flyer, a facsimile of the voting paper. It read: 'For Mayor – Honourable Pulvapies'.

When the votes were counted they realized the effectiveness of their advertising. The 4100 residents of the coastal town of Picoaza had elected 'The Honourable Pulvapies' mayor by a landslide majority.

THE BIG LIE

'All governments are liars', according to I.F. Stone, veteran US political commentator, 'We must believe nothing they say.' And yet they keep on saying it, and we, for our sins, seem to believe – at least a little.

Better Dead Than. . .

In May 1902 it was becoming starkly obvious to the citizens of St Pierre, the capital of Martinique, that their long-dormant volcano Mont Pelée was about to erupt. Each day people were being swallowed up by gaping fissures and drowned in gouts of boiling mud. When a hundred lethal fer-de-lance snakes, driven down the mountain by the hot ash, invaded the city and killed 50 people within an hour, the sensible thing appeared to many to be evacuation.

However, the Governor of Martinique, Louis Mouttet, had his eyes firmly fixed on the forthcoming elections and was loathe to let even one potential supporter slip away. Through his control of the local paper, Mouttet mounted a campaign to play down the danger, even organizing an excursion to the summit to 'see the fireworks'.

When, on May 5th, a wall of mud rose up and wiped out a sugar refinery, killing 159 people, he hastily set up a Commission of Inquiry, which even more hastly pronounced that: 'The safety of St Pierre is absolutely assured.' When, next day, red-hot cinders showered down on their rooftops, the Mayor issued a stern proclamation to his citizens: 'Do not allow yourselves to fall victims to groundless panic. Please allow us to advise you to return to your normal occupations.'

At dawn on May 8th, Mont Pelée erupted, obliterating St Pierre and wiping out its entire population of 30,000 – except for two men – a cobbler who hid in his cellar and a murderer who was being held in a cell on Death Row.

Father Knows Best

Grover Cleveland, President of the United States, in 1905: 'Sensible and responsible women do not want to vote. The relative positions to be assumed by man and woman in the working out of our civilization were assigned long ago by a higher intelligence than ours.'

You Never Had It So Good

Another American President, Herbert Hoover, was even further from the mark when he declared in 1928: 'We in America today are nearer the final triumph over poverty than ever before in the history of the land.' The next year the Stock Market crashed and ushered in the Great Depression.

Flower Power?

Dr Josef Goebbels, a bright new Nazi star on the German political scene, speaking in 1936: 'We rule by love and not by the bayonet.'

The Un-American Way

In 1938 the House Un-American Activities Committee was launched with a fanfare of righteousness: 'We shall be fair and impartial at all times and treat every witness with fairness and courtesy. We shall expect every witness to treat us in the same way. The Committee will not permit any character assassinations or any smearing of innocent people. . .'

It was, of course, this self-same Committee which was to destroy so many innocent victims during the 1950s and was to prove a useful tool to such character assassins as Senator Joe McCarthy.

All In Good Time

In 1939, with Europe simmering on the brink of war, British Prime Minister Neville Chamberlain saw himself as the oil on troubled waters. On July 27th he announced blandly: 'The Government has no reason to suppose that if grave events should supervene they should supervene in a fortnight, or three weeks, or any particular time.' How about five weeks?

A Matter of Definition

Even blander was Sir Anthony Eden, speaking in 1956 during the Suez Crisis: 'We are not at war with Egypt, we are in an armed conflict.'

Comrades. . .

Apparently 1956 was a good year for bogus reassurances. In that year Dr Hewlett Johnson – known to readers of the popular press as 'The Red Dean' – assured his parishioners: 'Russia could make the most appalling weapons, but she does not want to.' No doubt the *Daily Worker* would have concurred, judging by this snippet of 'Newspeak' during the Soviet takeover of Hungary later that same year: 'The Soviet troops are assisting the Hungarian people to retain their independence from Imperialism.'

No More Problems

Not so much a Big Lie as a Big Boast was the statement made by China's Foreign Minister, Chen Yi, in 1961: 'We do not want to sound immodest, but I can say that if China is admitted to the UN, then world affairs will be positively settled.'

Getting Dizzy

Harold Wilson, British Prime Minister, in 1966: 'Britain is swinging, but swinging into action, not decay.'

Who Is He Kidding?

Ian Smith, Rhodesian Prime Minister, in 1967: 'I think Rhodesia is a model for the rest of the world so far as race relations are concerned. I know of no happier country.'

Not Too Secret

In 1967, the head of the Russian KGB, Mr Andropov, made this rather disingenuous statement: 'Only enemies of the Soviet Union can think of the KGB as some sort of secret police.'

The Agony and the Ecstasy

In 1968, Democratic Presidential aspirant Hubert Humphrey told an auditorium full of cheering supporters: 'Here we are, the way politics ought to be in America. The politics of happiness . . . the politics of joy . . . and that's the way it's going to be from here on out.' Four months later the Democratic Convention in Chicago erupted into a baton-swinging free-for-all in which demonstrators battled Mayor Richard Daley's police, and the police battled reporters.

Pay Freeze

Just to show that politicians suffered too, California Governor Ronald Reagan assembled a press conference in 1968 to inform his constituents that: 'Taxes should hurt. I just mailed my own tax return last night, and I am prepared to say "Ouch" as loud as anyone.' A few years later, investigative reporting revealed that the Governor's pain was sometimes less than crippling. Through a series of legalistic sleights of hand, Reagan had avoided paying any tax at all for the whole of 1970.

More for Later

Anthony Wedgwood Benn, in 1968: 'We thought we could put the economy right in five years. We were wrong. It will probably take ten.'

Pineapple Pol

'I would prefer trying to grow pineapples in Alaska to being Chancellor of West Germany.' So said Franz Josef Strauss in 1968. 'I hope the German people are never so desperate as to believe they have to elect me as Chancellor.' So said Franz Josef Strauss in 1971.

'I am not a candidate for Chancellor under present political circumstances,' So said Franz Josef Strauss in April 1979.

In 1980 Franz Josef Strauss ran for Chancellor. He lost.

Not So Hot

Rev Ian Paisley, 1969: 'I've never made an inflammatory statement in my life.'

Going Up?

Roy Carr, Britain's Employment Secretary, speaking in October 1971 when the jobless figures were 929,121: 'The lights have turned from red to green.' Two months later the number of unemployed had risen to 966,802.

Simple Pleasures

Rhodesian Prime Minister Ian Smith, in 1971: 'We have the happiest Africans in the world.'

Shock Horror!

During the 1972 American presidential election, Vice-Presidential candidate Tom Eagleton came under withering fire after he revealed that he had once undergone electric shock treatment for mental illness. Attempting to squash the furor, Eagleton's presidential running mate, George McGovern, announced. 'I am one thousand per cent for Tom Eagleton and have no intention of dropping him from the ticket.' A few days later he dropped Eagleton from the ticket.

Too Much

Ronald Reagan, 1973: 'The thought of being President frightens me and I do not think I want the job.'

We Try Harder

Joe Gormley, President of the National Union of Miners, when on record with this gem in February 1973: 'For one union to take on the Government this year would be damned suicide.' That winter, Gormley's miners single-handedly took on the Heath Government, and toppled it.

Who's Leaving?

In January 1974 Enoch Powell said in an interview: 'I am the last person whom it would be reasonable to expect to leave the [Conservative] Party.' He then promptly quit to join the Ulster Unionists.

No Change

Ian Smith, Rhodesian Prime Minister, 1975: 'There are going to be no dramatic changes in Rhodesia.'

The Old Gang

In 1976, Jimmy Carter's aide Hamilton Jordan made this campaign promise: 'If, after the Inauguration, you find a Cy Vance as Secretary of State and Zbigniew Brzezinski as Head of National Security, then I would say we failed. And I'd quit.' They were, but he didn't.

How About a Fourth?

Shirley Williams, May 25, 1980: 'I am not interested in a third party. I do not believe that it has any future.

You Don't Say

Libya's leader Colonel Muammar Gaddafi, speaking in *Newsweek* in April, 1979: 'I love peace.' In January 1981 he invaded and annexed neighbouring Chad.

Tass, the Soviet news agency, in April 1980: 'The gratitude of all honest Afghans to Soviet troops is that of sincere hospitality and profound gratitude.'

WAS MY FACE RED!

Or, in the words of the late American Politician Hubert Humphrey: 'I say some things and, gosh, I wish I hadn't said them.'

We Were Wondering About That

Ronald Reagan, in a speech designed to put America on better terms with developing countries. 'The United States has much to offer the third world war.' (He went on to repeat the error nine times during the course of the speech.)

Was There A Man Dismayed?

Lord Airey, in a handwritten note to his Light Brigade at Balaclava: 'Lord Raglan wishes the cavalry to advance rapidly to the front, follow the enemy and try to prevent the enemy carrying away the guns. Troop horse artillery may accompany. French cavalry is on your left. Immediate.'

The Light Brigade received the note and charged – in the wrong direction. Out of the 700 horsemen, only 195 returned in one piece.

Say Goodnight, Don

'Uncle Don' Carney was Radio WOR-New York's bedtime storyteller during the 1920s. But his career ended abruptly one night when, assuming the microphone to be dead, he signed off to his engineer – and unwittingly to his large pre-teen audience as well – with the words: 'There, I guess that'll hold the little bastards for another night!'

White House Follies

Gerald Ford, during his television debate with Jimmy Carter during the 1976 election campaign: 'There is no Soviet domination of Eastern Europe, and there never will be under a Ford administration.' After *that*, there was no Ford administration, either.

Wrong Church

During the Middle East war of 1948, the US ambassador to the UN, Warren Austin, called upon the warring Arabs and Jews to settle their differences 'like good Christians'.

Wrong Enemy

During the Spanish-American War, Confederate veteran General Joe Wheeler caused some confusion amongst his ranks when, during the storming of Las Guasimas, he roared: 'Come on, boys! we've got the damn Yankees on the run!'

Knee Deep

The biggest event on the Penzance and Zennor Sub Aqua Club's 1979 calendar was an excursion to Scotland's Loch Buidhe. Said Chairman Stanley Tees before setting out: 'We're all looking forward to diving in Loch Buidhe.' With that the club members drove north for 700 miles, climed 3000 feet into the Highlands, changed into its scuba gear and dived in. They then discovered that Loch Buidhe is only six inches deep. Confessed Mr Tees Later: 'We all felt very depressed.'

Redistribute the Weapons

Observed Hubert Humphrey after would-be assassin Sarah Jane Moore bungled her attempt to shoot President Gerald Ford: 'There are too many guns in the hands of people who don't know how to use them!'

Don't Call Us. . .

In 1975 a man rang the police in Eureka, California. He told them 'A noisy drunken man is creating a disturbance at a call box.' He gave the address and added a description: 'He's 6 feet tall, 190 pounds, blue eyes, white hat, red coat.' The police cruiser arrived at the call box to find a helpless drunk sitting by it. He had given them a perfect description of himself.

Jackson Six

Mistaking talk-show host Michael Jackson of KABC-radio Los Angeles for one of the Jackson Five, Ted Kennedy gushed: 'The music of you and your brothers has been an inspiration to millions.' After a bemused pause, Jackson replied: 'Sir, I shall try to keep talking with natural rhythm.'

Forty-eight Times No

Wendell Wilkie, US Presidential candidate, at a dinner on December 7, 1941, after a guest had predicted that America would be at war with Japan within forty-eight hours: 'We won't be at war with Japan within forty-eight hours, within forty-eight days. within forty-eight years.' At that precise moment the telephone rang, and the guests were informed that the Japanese had bombed Pearl Harbour.

Hat Check

In 1967 an irate Minneapolis judge, sensitive to any disrespect towards the Bench, ordered: 'That man wearing a hat in my courtroom. Get out of here at once!' The culprit rose and left without a murmur. It was several minutes before someone realised that he had been awaiting trial on burglary charges.

White House Follies (2)

Gerald Ford proposing a toast during a banquet given in his honour by Egyptian President Anwar Sadat: 'To the great people and the Government of Israel. . . excuse me, of Egypt.'

Germs Can Kill

During Napoleon III's *coup d'etat* of 1851, an excited aide burst in to report to Count St Arnaud that an ugly mob had assembled outside and was menacing the Imperial Guard. The Count had his own problems, notably a bad sore throat. '*Ma sacrée toux!*' (My damned cough!) he muttered to himself. Thinking that the Count had said 'Massacrez tous!' (Massacre the lot!), the aide duly scurried off to give the order. Thousands died.

Mr Butz Goes to Washington

Although enjoying the exalted position of American Secretary of Agriculture, Earl Butz was really just a good ol' boy from down on the farm. In 1976, while jetting to a speaking engagement, Earl buttonholed former Nixon aide John Dean and joked, 'Coloureds want only three things: first, a tight pussy; second, loose shoes; and third, a warm place to shit.' Dean dutifully slapped his thigh and then went away and printed Earl's quip. Soon after, Earl resigned.

Colour Blind

When Mario Procaccino, Democratic candidate for mayor of New York, canvassed a group of black voters in 1969, he stunned them with: 'My heart is as black as yours.'

Third Rater

October 1953 was not a good month for radio personality Gilbert Harding. Speaking to a dinner given by the Hounslow Magistrates on the 6th, he informed them: 'I have been dragged along to this third-rate place for a third-rate dinner for third-rate people.' When the magistrates had digested this information, there was uproar. The next day he apologized: 'I behaved abominably.' The day after that, Harding attended the premiere of *The King and I*, a musical starring

Valerie Hobson. Harding slept through the performance; his critical response did not please the cast. He apologized again: 'I'm sorry, I've had a tiring day.'

Mini Leap

In order to boost their finances, the Droylsden Football Club of Manchester voted to engage stuntman Paddy Jones and his Irish Daredevils. Paddy's show promised a gripping climax, 'a death-defying leap over fourteen cars.'

'I can do it', said Paddy. Unfortunately, only five of the promised fourteen cars could be found. The rest, said Paddy, had to be imagined. Then he climed into his racing Mini, roared up a ramp at 20 miles an hour, and nose-dived into the second car in the line. The football club refunded the two hundred disgruntled spectators' money.

Later they discovered they had actually lost money on the event, having paid back money to a number of children who had sneaked into the ground without paying.

Bound for Glory

One of the most famous pieces of correspondence to come out of the American Civil War was Abraham Lincoln's consolatory letter to Mrs Lydia Bixby. Wrote the Great Man: 'You are the mother of five sons who have died gloriously on the field of battle.'

The facts, however, were somewhat different. Two of her sons *were* killed in battle, but the third was captured at Gettysburg and later swapped in a prisoner exchange, a fourth deserted to join the Confederates, and the fifth deserted and fled to Cuba. Mrs Bixby herself was an active pacifist who had attempted to dissuade all her sons from signing up.

Rolling In The Aisles

The Rev Yeomans of Pontesbury found his congregation singing the hymn 'I Cannot Help But Wonder Where I'm Bound' in what he considered a dull and lifeless manner. So the vivacious vicar decided to liven them up by dancing in the aisles. They had barely reached the second verse when the Reverend, arms waving in true Holy Roller ecstasy, plunged through the weakened floor and disappeared into the central heating system.

Fun and Games

When New York mayor John F. Hylan decided to defend the police during a crime wave in 1922, there were no doubt many officers who wished he hadn't. 'The police', said Hylan, 'are fully able to meet and compete with the criminals.'

Lightning Strikes

When asked about the possibility of lightning striking an aircraft, Boeing's Donald Nordstrom, designer of the 707, scoffed: 'To my knowledge there have never been any fires occurring as a result of such strikes.' In December 1963, Pan Am Clipper 214 was hit by lightning and plunged to earth on the outskirts of Washington DC. Eighty-one crew and passengers lost their lives.

White House Follies (3)

Gerald Ford: 'When a man is asked to make a speech, the first thing he has to decide is what to say.'

The Long Goodbye

Russian ruler Paul I was known – with some reason – as the Mad Czar. Reviewing his troops one day in 1799, he spotted a dirty button on a soldier's coat. Livid with rage, he ordered the squad: 'About turn! Quick march!'

'Where to, Majesty?' asked the commanding officer. 'To Siberia!' snapped the Czar. Without hesitation, 400 crack Russian troops set out on the 2000-mile trek across the Russian wastes. They were never seen again.

Ayatollah So!

Wary about their increasingly awkward position as front men for an internationally unpopular regime, the Ayatollah's Iranian Embassy staff in London requested additional police protection. Replied Scotland Yard's Embassy Protection Officer, R. Bromley: 'I assure you that your embassy will receive the closest attention at all times.'

Days later, dissident Iranians invaded and settled in for Britain's first-ever embassy seige.

The Wages of Gin

In 1920, Commissioner John F. Kramer, unveiling a new US law that would become known as Prohibition: 'This law will be obeyed in cities, large and small, and in villages, and where it is not obeyed it will be enforced. The law says that liquor to be used as a beverage must not be manufactured. We shall see that it is not manufactured. Nor sold, nor given away, nor hauled in anything on the surface of the earth, or under the earth, or in the air.'

Horsing Around

Dale Evans, wife of Hollywood's cowboy star Roy Rogers: 'In horse vernacular, Roy has always "given me my head", and I have tried to do the same for him.'

Law and Order

After the bloody 1968 Democratic Convention in Chicago, Mayor Richard Daley defended his controversial police force with: 'Get this thing straight once and for all. The policeman isn't there to create disorder. The policeman is there to preserve disorder.'

White House Follies (4)

Gerald Ford: 'I say that if Lincoln were living today he would turn over in his grave!'

Teller Like It Is

Acting on a tip-off, Atlanta Georgia's police chief ordered his men to stake out a local bank which they did, much to the consternation of the branch manager. After suffering their presence for a time, the manager could stand it no longer.

'Please leave', he implored the officers. 'Your presence is disturbing employees and customers.' Obligingly, they left. Five minutes later the bank was robbed.

In The Eye Of The Beholder

Maine's Hayes E. Gahagan was one of 1978's more conservative Senate candidates, and he made no bones about it. Anti-abortion, anti-women's rights, Gahagan declared: 'The vote I'm after is the Christian patriot.'

He failed to notice that his campaign photographs had been cunningly doctored to display a picture of a vagina interspersed with his hair, and the word 'SEX' was etched into the shadow of his right eyebrow and below the knuckles of his left hand. He lost the election.

A Bit Nippy

In Pittsburgh in 1976, KDKA-TV's announcer kicked off the nightly news with: 'In the headlines: Emperor Hirohito rides in an open carriage to Williamsburg . . . and our weatherman, Bob Kudzma, says there's a nip in the air.'

Good Grief—It's Hubby!

Bored West German housefrau Ilsa Schmidt decided to spice up her sex life by placing an advertisement in a local contact magazine: 'Sex kitten seeks sharp cat! Send candid pictures!' Among the many replies she received was one from her husband Klaus. After recovering from the shock, Ilsa filed for divorce, claiming that this was the first time she had seen her husband naked. Apparently he had always insisted on making love to her with the lights out.

White House Follies (5)

Gerald Ford: 'I'm a great fan of baseball. I watch a lot of games on the radio. Er, I mean television.'

You Said It

In a speech during the Watergate scandal in 1974, Richard Nixon informed a bemused TV audience: 'This is a discredited president.' (He meant 'precedent'.)

Blast!!

Lord Glasgow (1874-1963) was an accommodating old squire who thought nothing of allowing the local Commando Corps to use his extensive estate for manoeuvres. Naturally enough, the commandos wished to be accommodating in return, so they volunteered their services to help blow up an old tree stump on his property. Lord Glasgow was delighted; his only reservation was that the plantation of young saplings growing nearby might be injured.

'No, no', Colonel Durnford Slater assured him, 'We can blow a tree down so it falls on a sixpence!' 'My', marvelled the good Lord, 'you are clever!' The Colonel instructed his subaltern to prepare the explosives – 75 pounds in all. 'Is that enough?' queried the Colonel. 'Yessir!' replied the subaltern. 'Exactly right. I worked it out by mathematics.' Just to be on the safe side, the Colonel had him add a few pounds more.

After a good lunch everyone trooped out to witness the exercise. Said the Colonel proudly to his Lordship: 'You will see that tree fall flat at just that angle where it will hurt no young trees!' Whereupon he lit the fuse, and retired.

Seconds later the stump rose fifty feet into the air, taking with it half an acre of soil and the entire plantation of saplings. 'I made a mistake', stammered the subaltern. 'It should have been 7.5 pounds, not 75.'

A saddened Lord Glasgow walked back to his castle in silence. Rounding a turn in the drive, he found every pane of glass in the building was broken. Uttering a little cry, the distraught Lord fled to the lavatory to hide his sorrow like a gentleman. When he pulled the chain, the entire ceiling, loosened by the blast, came down on his head.

Where There's Hope

Defending the hapless Spiro Agnew in 1973, Texas Governor John Connally blurted: 'I hope that Spiro Agnew will be completely exonerated and found guilty of the charges against him.'

Heavenly Days

Andrew Young, US ambassador to the United Nations, speaking soon after the revolution in Iran: 'Ayatollah Khomeini will one day be viewed as some kind of a saint.'

Jesus Wept!

'The most famous pair of stablemates since Joseph and Mary' was how WNBC-TV sportscaster Dick Schaap described racehorses Secretariat and Riva Ridge in 1975. The crack jammed the switchboard with 900 complainants. Schaap apologized.

White House Follies (6)

Gerald Ford: 'Mr Nixon was the thirty-seventh President of the United States. He had been preceded by thirty-six others.'

JUST PLAIN DICK

Politicians are simply defined: at best they are duplicitous, and at worst they lie. For all the rhetoric, the words of *Washington Post* journalist David Broder, talking here of the US Presidency but also generally applicable, tell the story: 'Anyone who wants the job badly enough to do what must be done to obtain it should not be trusted with it.' Few escape that condemnation. Others, of course, infinitely surpass it. For most, lying is merely an inescapable part of their careers; others build their careers on lying. Ex-President Richard Milhous Nixon could be considered a member of that dubious elect. Indeed, he could be called its maestro.

The chapter title refers to the headline given by showbiz magazine *Variety* to Richard Nixon's 1952 'Checkers' Speech, echoing a currently popular soap opera entitled *Just Plain Bill*.

Youthful Ambition

In 1925, aged 12, Richard Nixon told his mother Hannah: 'Mother, I want to be an old-fashioned lawyer, an honest lawyer who can't be bought by crooks.'

Prize-Winner

In 1928, aged 15, speaking at a school debate: 'We must defend our Constitution against a great wave of indifference to authority, disrespect of its law, and opposition to its basic principles which threatens its basic existence. Shall we of the

131

present generation allow this instrument to be cast into disrepute? Shall we be responsible for its downfall?'

Nixon won $30 for this essay in ironic prophecy.

No Experience Required

In 1946 the local Republican Party required new blood. They placed this ad in the local paper in Whittier, California, Nixon's birthplace: 'Wanted: Congressman candidate with no previous political experience to defeat a man who has represented the district in the House for ten years. Any young man, resident of the district, preferably a veteran, fair education, may apply for the job.'

They netted Richard Nixon. He beat Jerry Voorhis, the incumbent, by smearing him as a Communist.

'I'm Not a Quitter'

General Eisenhower picked Nixon as his Vice Presidential running mate for the 1952 election. In September Nixon was accused of using an $18,000 'slush' fund for his own use. He appeared on NBC-TV, with over 800 local affiliated stations, in what was described as a 'soap opera'. He manipulated his audience with sentimentality, speaking of a dog called 'Checkers' which had been given to his family and of his wife Pat's 'good Republican cloth coat'. He assured his audience: 'I'm going to campaign up and down America until we drove (sic) the crocks and the Communists and those that defend them out of Washington.'

He added: 'I'm not a quitter and incidentally Pat's not a quitter. After all, her name was Patricia Ryan and she was born on St Patrick's Day.' In fact Pat Nixon was born on March 16. St Patrick's Day is March 17.

On September 14, 1955, at a lunch for the Radio and Television Executives Society, Nixon revealed: 'You'll remember the "Checkers" speech, I suppose. Well, I want you to be the first to know . . . I staged it. I'm a firm believer in "off-the-cuff" speeches that take a lot of time to prepare.'

132

Setting it Straight

On September 18, 1956, while electioneering for his and Eisenhower's second term, Nixon said, 'Let's get one thing straight right now: where our opponents misrepresent and distort the record and where they vilify the President of the United States, I shall consider it a duty and a privilege to set the record straight.'

Fighting Talk

Nixon in 1958: 'Win or lose, it is unforgivable to lack the courage to fight for the principles we believe in.'

He Who Laughs Last

In 1960, debating with his opponent for the Presidency, John F. Kennedy, on nationwide television, Nixon claimed: 'Whenever any mother or father talks to his (sic) child, I hope he can look at the man in the White House and, whatever he may think of his politics, he will say, "Well, there is a man who maintains the kind of standards personally that I would want my child to follow".'

Kennedy just laughed, long and loud.

Softly As I Leave You

Having lost in 1960, Nixon tried to defeat California Governor Pat Brown two years later. He lost again. On November 7, 1962, he spoke to the press: 'As I leave . . . all I can say is this: for sixteen years . . . you've had a lot of fun, you had opportunities to attack me . . . Just think about how much you're going to be missing, you won't have Nixon to kick around anymore because, gentlemen, this is my last press conference.'

He then added, 'I hope that what I've said today will at least make the TV, radio and press recognize the great responsibility that they have to report all the news and, second, to recognize that they have the right and a responsibility, if they're against a candidate, to give him the shaft.'

During the Johnson administration Nixon began to feel a slight itch. It was campaign time again: 'The press are good guys, I have a lot of friends in the press . . . I like the press because basically I'm like them, because of my own inquisitiveness. The press are very helpful with their questions.'

To Tell the Truth (1)

On August 8, 1968, Nixon accepted the Republican Presidential nomination: 'Let us begin by committing ourselves to the truth, to see it like it is and to tell it like it is; to find the truth, to speak the truth and to live with the truth. That is what we will do.'

In November, having beaten Hubert Humphrey, he became America's 37th President: 'Winning is a lot more fun. I won without having to pay the price or make any deals.'

When You've Got It

Nixon described his Vice-President, Spiro T. Agnew, former Governor of Maryland, in 1968: 'There can be a mystique about a man. You can look him in the eye and know he's got it. This guy has got it.'

Vice-President Agnew responded: 'I promise that truth shall be the policy of the Nixon-Agnew administration.'

Disaster Prone

The President's future right-hand man, Henry Kissinger, former Harvard professor and nuclear theorist, remarked just before Nixon won the election: 'Of all the men running, Richard Nixon is the most dangerous to have as President. I would never work for that man. That man is a disaster.' Kissinger joined the Nixon team soon afterwards.

To Tell the Truth (2)

Later that year, the Vice-President added: 'A Nixon-Agnew adminstration will abolish the credibility gap and re-establish the truth, the whole truth, as its policy.'

And for any faint hearts, the ultra-right-wing Senator Strom Thurmond of South Carolina produced posters declaring: 'Strom Says You Can Trust Dick.'

In 1969 Herb Klein, Nixon's Director of Communications, intoned: 'Truth will become the hallmark of the Nixon Administration . . . It will eliminate any possibility of a credibility gap.' And Spiro Agnew again chipped in his mite: 'After all, what does a politician have but his credibility?'

In 1972 UK journalist George Gale wrote in the May issue of *Harper's Magazine:* 'At worst Nixon is likely to be the best of a bad lot. At the best he could become the greatest of the post-war presidents.'

Water-bugging (1)

A May 1972 headline over a story about President Nixon opined: 'No One Knows What He Might Do'.

On June 17, Frank Wills, a guard, was checking on the suite containing the Democratic National Committee headquarters in the Watergate complex in Washington DC. He noticed some tape holding back a lock, and called the police. . .

On June 18, 1972, Waterbugger Howard Hunt remarked to a colleague: 'Everything is under control. Everything will be taken care of. Those people will say nothing. There will be no damage done to the campaign.' Meanwhile Nixon's supporters chanted their campaign slogan: 'Four More Years!'

On August 29, 1972, the President (advised by John Dean, his own counsel), made his position clear on the Watergate break-in: 'Within our own staff, under my direction, Counsel to the President Mr Dean has conducted a complete investigation of all leads which might involve any present members of the White House or anybody in Government. I can say categorically that . . . no one in the White House staff, no one in this administration, presently employed, was involved in this bizarre incident.'

Who Can Say?

When the London *Times* summed up the year 1972, Louis Heren wrote: 'Once again Mr Nixon demonstrated flexibility and what must be described as adventurism. Who can doubt that he is contemplating a few more surprises for the new year.'

And on January 9, 1973, Nixon was 60 years old. 'I expect the first four years of my sixties to be very interesting. I hope to do great things.'

Water-bugging (2)

On February 28, 1973, John Dean explained to a worried President: 'We've made it this far and I'm convinced that we are going to make it the whole road and put this thing in the funny pages of the history books.'

On March 21, Dean added: 'I can give a show we can sell them, just like we were selling Wheaties.'

But Watergate refused to go away. The *Washington Post* duo of Woodward and Bernstein were probing. The trail of the secret dirty-tricks team – 'the Plumbers' – was approaching the Oval Office. On April 30, 1973, Nixon addressed the nation, flanked by a bust of Lincoln and pictures of Pat and the kids. His top aides, Bob Haldeman and John Erlichman – '. . . two of the finest public servants it had been my privilege to know. . .' – were sacked.

Nixon promised: 'There will be no whitewash at the White House', and urged the press: 'Gentlemen, we have had our disagreements in the past, and I hope you give me hell every time I am wrong.' He also set a high moral tone: 'I reject the cynical view that politics is inevitably, or even usually dirty business.'

Agnew added his bit: 'We are inundated with rumour, hearsay, Grand Jury leaks, speculation and statements from undisclosed sources. It is entirely possible that some of this may be proven later to be accurate.'

Pardon My Language

In August 1973 an investigation began, linking Vice-President Agnew to financial finagling in his home state of Maryland: 'The charges against me are, if you'll pardon the expression, damned lies. I am innocent of these charges. If indicted I will not resign.' On October 10, however, Agnew duly resigned, to be replaced by Gerald Ford, Spiro blamed what he still claims were minor peccadilloes on 'this post-Watergate morality', and he has written a *roman à clef*.

On July 13, 1973, a White House staffer blithely revealed Nixon's tape-recording system, which monitored all Oval Office conversations. The President's attitude was: 'I may be bothered about the taping equipment, but I'm damn glad we have it.'

Summing Up

Nixon in August 1973: 'The time has come to turn Watergate over to the courts.'

September: 'Watergate is water under the bridge.'

November: 'I am not a crook.' On another occasion he admitted, 'I would not be candid if I did not admit that this has not been an easy year in some respects.'

The Final Solution

In January 1974 Nixon presented his annual State of the Union speech. Alas, the Freudian slip must out: 'I urge the Congress to join me in mounting a major new effort to replace the discredited President.'

February: 'I do not expect to be impeached.'

March: Vice-President Ford, in the tradition of his predecessor, stood four-square behind his leader: 'I know of no more bombshells, I don't think there will be any.'

Nixon, in July: 'If these charges were true, nobody would have to ask me to resign. I wouldn't serve for one minute if they were true.'

A month later the White House Tapes were in the public domain. Nixon's comment: 'My own view is that taping of conversations for historical purposes was a bad thing . . . Portions of the tapes of these . . . conversations are at variance with certain of my previous statements . . . I recognize that this . . . may further damage my case.'

Later that month he reiterated: 'I have no intention of resigning. The President is not going to leave the White house until January 20, 1977.'

On August 8, 1974, six years to the day after accepting the nomination that brought him his first term as President, Nixon resigned.

The next day, Nixon revived the shade of 'Checkers' with a mawkish farewell speech to his staff. The old style continued: 'This country needs good farmers, good businessmen, good plumbers. . .'

LIKELY STORIES

Explaining away criticism is a universal response to being blamed. But sometimes the resulting excuse may have the speaker wishing that he hadn't said anything after all.

The Ear Nose

Addison Mizner, the eccentric society architect of 1920s America, was once caught playing pinochle during a piano recital organized by the formidable doyenne of the Florida set, Mrs Edward T. Stotesbury. When the enraged dowager demanded an explanation, Mizner murmured apologetically. 'I thought it was the piano tuner.'

Outside Office Hours

When East Kent police discovered an unemployed labourer in a Cliftonville bank late one October evening, they (not unnaturally) asked him what he was up to. 'I've come about my overdraft', was his reply.

Don't Apollo-gize

After being scolded by a friend who had caught her *in flagrante delicto* with her chauffeur, dancer Isadora Duncan sniffed by way of explanation: 'He's a Greek god in disguise.'

Gone With The Wind

Less cruel but equally phony was the promise of another US boxing manager, Angelo Dundee, to his 'boy' in 1965. After eight hard rounds, the fighter gasped to Dundee that his legs were killing him. 'That's a very good sign', said Dundee knowingly. 'It means you're getting your second wind!'

Axe for a Drink

When asked by the court why he had buried a hatchet in the bar of the Scotia Lounge, Murray Clyde of Aberdeen explained: 'I was having difficulty in catching the barmaid's eye.'

Alias Smith and Jones

Political Science student Alan Smith confessed to Hartlepool magistrates that he had indeed given a false name to police when they had arrested him. Explained Smith: 'I didn't think they would believe my name was Smith because I had no identification on me, so I told them it was Jones.'

Recycling Energy

A Bangor man, who confessed to using the same one coin in the gas from the meter at his home for nearly a year, pleaded with magistrates that he had done it 'on the spur of the moment'.

Secret Ingredient

In December 1980, Missouri mental hospital escapee Thaddeus Lipscomb was charged with robbing a fried chicken stand in Little Rock, Arkansas. Williams told doctors who questioned him after his arrest: 'I heard voices telling me that if I did certain things I could marry Diana Ross.'

More Medicine

The Bradford *Telegraph and Argus* reported the tragic case of Laurie Marsh, who was appearing before the Bradford City Court charged with being drunk. When asked by the Court Chairman what he had to say for himself, Mr Marsh replied: 'I have just come out of hospital where I have been having treatment for my drinking.'

See No Evil

The *Evening Echo* reported that a 48-year-old Southend woman had been arrested for prostitution. In her defence, the unfortunate woman told the Southend magistrates that she was too short-sighted to ply for trade, being blind in one eye and suffering blurred vision in the other. 'I can only see if someone is right on top of me', she added.

Overdue

While firemen were sifting through the aftermath of a fire in a New York City building, they discovered in an adjoining apartment 15,000 New York Public Library books. Stolen over a period of ten years, the books were piled to the ceiling and covered every square inch of floor space. It took twenty men and seven trucks three days to move them.

The owner of the apartment, a 58-year-old New York lawyer, was subsequently charged with theft. 'I like to read', he explained.

Cold Winds in Hell

In November 1980, a nun was arrested in a London department store and charged with shoplifting. She told the bench that it was 'the work of the Devil' that two cardigans were found in her handbag.

Bird Brain

When arrested and charged with bird smuggling, the captain of a New Zealand yacht explained away the presence of a cockatoo under his bunk with: 'I was sailing from Fiji to Wellington when the bird flew into the mast and fell stunned into the cabin.' When asked why a case of birdseed was also discovered under the bunk, he replied: 'My wife and I like it sprinkled on our junket.'

Home is Where the Heart Is

Arrested for urinating in a public place, a Plaistow man protested his innocence in court, He had, he said, pinned a notice to a nearby tree which read GENTLEMEN. 'I always carry it with me in case of need', he explained.

I Must So You Won't

Black religious leader Father Divine (alias George Baker and God) ruled that the thousands of converts to his Peace Mission Movement should remain celibate, even if they were already married. In 1931 Divine was arrested on Long Island for living with a woman who was not his wife. During the furor it was revealed that he had seduced a long line of nubile followers. His explanation: 'I am bringing your desire to the surface so that I can eliminate it.'

Water Worker

Charged with indecent exposure, Robert Butler told an English court: 'I was brought up in Nigeria, and when the consequences of the drought became obvious I decided to put the national interest first and perform the *n'dula,* a naked rain dance, on the village green. That night the rain began and continued for twenty-four hours. I estimate that up to £500,000 worth of crops were saved.' He was fined £10.

Dog Day Afternoon

Charged with the cultivation of 'over 200' cannabis plants in his back yard, Phillip Tenby had a ready explanation. He had been on his way to buy a parrot when he had suddenly realized that if he planted a packet of sunflower seeds first, he would have a life-long supply of birdseed once the bird arrived. However, after the seeds began to sprout they were so pleased with their handiwork that he and his wife Sandra agreed to forget the parrot and concentrate on gardening.

Asked by the magistrates why, when the police had burst in, Sandra Tenby had been discovered furiously uprooting the three-foot-high plants and hurling them into her neighbour's back yard, she replied: 'I had decided to get a dog.'

Academic Discipline

Arrested and charged with soliciting a Sydney policewoman for prostitution, Brian Caulfield explained that he and his friend Robert Rolf were 'both keen sociology students finishing an all-Australia study of sex-tariffs'.

Sales Force

'I suppose we all got a little excited because business had been so bad', was how Nottinghamshire car dealer J. J. Rowe explained his treatment of a potential customer. When the man decided against an exchange deal at the last moment, Mr Rowe held his elbow while he tried to persuade him to sign. Then, when the startled customer attempted to climb out through the window, Mr Rowe's four sons entered the office and sat on him while their father once more outlined the bargain the man was passing up.

Good Samaritan

When Peter Smith, a trainee flight controller, was charged with stealing a glass from a local pub, he said: 'I am definitely not guilty. Making my way home from the control tower I saw a man standing in the street with a glass of beer in his hand. He told me that the glass was stuck to his hand and asked me to help him get free of it. When I had done so he gave me the glass and its contents by way of a reward.' The court fined him £5.

Handling Money

When Miss Claudine Tousel of Alencon, a bank employee, appeared before a local court charged with stealing money from her place of employment, she laid the blame squarely on her boyfriend Ermis. Said Miss Tousel: 'I know men like women with big ones, so I filled up my brassiére with notes. Ermis was fondling me behind the bank when he suddenly remembered an important engagement. I never saw him again.' On further questioning the court learned she had known Ermis for 'about fifteen minutes'.

A Hole Lot of Fun

Caught in the act of drilling a hole in the wall between the male and female lavatories, a church charity raffle organizer pleaded: 'I had just brought a Bumper Tool outfit and could not wait until I got home to try it out.'

Looking Good

Arrested for breaking and entering the Twintop Hair Salon in August 1965, and Oxford defendant claimed: 'I felt tired, so I rested my head against the shop window and it fell in.' When the court was further told that he had been caught wearing a fur coat belonging to the salon, he replied: 'I wore it to keep the dust off my sportscoat.'

Kiss Me Quick

Charged with stealing a kiss from a 42-year-old meter maid, a 77-year-old Cardiff defendant pleaded that he was 'a man subject to violent bouts of senility'.

A Hard Night's Work

Asked to explain her presence in the storeroom of a Glasgow bedding company at midnight with three men – two of whom were known burglars – Mrs June Withy, a 19-year-old widow, said: 'I was up for a wee shot on the swings.'

Testing, Testing. . .

In 1979, a Dutch optician was charged with various offences relating to his treatment of female clients. During the procedings it was alleged that when women visited his consulting rooms, they were told to remove their clothing and dance around while he played the accordian. 'This test was carried out to make sure that they were the right kind for contact lenses', explained his lawyer.

A Rest Cure

Charged with attempting to evade arrest, Don Orrin, manager of a local musical group told Brighton magistrates: 'I locked Elmer, our singer, in an amplifier chest. I could not open the chest when police came looking for him because Tenner, the group's dog, had swallowed the key,' Asked by police what he was doing in the chest, Elmer Jenkins replied: 'I was resting between engagements.' Both were fined.

Ho-ho-ho

When he was arrested on an English beach brandishing a chair leg studded with four-inch nails, an Iranian student happily informed the court in which he was charged with possession of an offensive weapon: 'This is no weapon. It is a bat used in the popular Arabian beach sport of *ho-ho*. The rules are similar to rounders.' Asked why, in this case, he was found up to his knees in sea-water during a violent snowstorm, he explained: 'The weather was unsuitable for *ho-ho*, so I decided to club a few fish.'

Snake Bite

Drawing up to some traffic lights in Morgantown, South Carolina, Mr Surling noticed that from the window of the car next to him protruded the tail of a python. This snake, named Mr Slippy, belonged to the car's driver, Ms Anderson.

Surling called over to ask whether he could touch the snake. Ms Anderson agreed, upon which Surling grabbed the tail, bit off an inch of it, spat it out and drove off. Charged later with damaging the snake, Surling informed the court: 'I am a jazz drummer; I must be free.' He was fined $5000.

Make Change Not War

Accused in 1978 of breaking into a contraceptive machine, a hapless bridegroom told the magistrate: 'It was our wedding night and my wife wouldn't let me get into bed until I had a contraceptive. Unfortunately neither of us had any change.'

Closer, My God, To Thee

In 1973 the Turin vice squad raided a massage parlour which, among other services, offered 'overall body massage with opportunities for meditation'. Using the passwords 'Peace and Goodwill', they surprised many customers, including a stark naked priest who was locked in 'deep meditation' with a 32-year-old masseuse. On the way to the cells he told the policemen: 'I needed this experience to understand the problems of my parishioners.'

Tory Tactics

Busted in 1973 for the possession of a quantity of cannabis, which officers had found in the seams of his trousers, the accused pleaded ignorance. 'I have no knowledge. The drug must have been where it was found when I bought the trousers – at a Conservative Party jumble sale.'

Our Feathered Friends

Invited to a fancy dress ball in Bedfordshire, one urban reveller suitably arrayed himself and set off for the country-side. There he lost his bearings but, chancing upon an open-air performance of 'A Midsummer Night's Dream', he cheered up.

'I had been wandering around the countryside for several hours. I thought I had arrived at last.' At this point, the court heard, dressed feather-perfect as a farmyard chicken, the defendant leapt onto the stage, flapped his wings and repeatedly exclaimed 'Ork!' several times. He was fined £10 for disturbing the peace.

Plat du Jour

Frenchman Noel Carriou faced trial in 1973 for murdering two successive wives. He told the judge: 'I killed the first because she undercooked my steak, and the second because she overcooked it.' Noting that 'the quality of cooking is an important part of marriage', the judge duly dropped the murder charges, although Carriou still went down for eight years for 'womanslaughter.'

Heat Stroke

In 1974, 19-year-old housewife Charlotte Tyler admitted to a grand jury that she had slept with some 5000 policemen in and around her home town of Memphis, Tennessee. Claiming that her sexual appetites were by no means voluntary, she told the court: 'I am bringing an action for $1,000,000 against a health spa. There, trapped for ninety minutes in the sauna, I changed from a devout Catholic housewife into a raving nymphomaniac.'

Her particular predilection for policemen was possibly 'something to do with my belief in law and order'. Mrs Tyler looked forward to a successful suit, having hired a special attorney, an expert in 'shock-induced behaviour switch', who had recently extracted $300,000 for a client whose cable car crash had left her similarly voracious.

Fruity

On trial in 1973 for 'molesting wild animals in a national park', the defendant, president of a Cape Angling Club in South Africa, explained: 'I had been driving about the park for nine days without seeing a single animal. Suddenly I saw a family of lions eating their kill. I became very excited, forgot myself, and pelted them with oranges from the window of my car.'

Sweet Shopped

Tossing a half-eaten Mars bar from the window of his truck, Cumberland van driver James Anderson hit and knocked out a passing professional wrestler, Neil Goldie. Accepting the £10 fine levied by the court for actual bodily harm, Anderson said, 'The Mars was giving me a toothache, so I thought it best to get rid of it.'

Don't Look Now

In 1974, seaborne customs officials picked up thirty-eight starving, sleepy refugees in a leaky boat lost in the Caribbean. The party were attempting to escape from Port-au-Prince in Haiti. All were blindfolded. A spokesman explained: 'We did not want them to witness their own destruction.'

Your Friendly Policeman

Hearing someone knocking on the side door of Hyde Park police station one night in 1974, Constable Weatherell duly opened it. He found a tramp who asked, 'Can I have a cup of tea?' The tramp found no tea, only arrest for begging.

In court he told the magistrate, 'I had no idea it was a police station. There was a light shining under the door and sounds of friendly cheer coming from behind it. The next thing I knew, I was in the cells.'

Christmas Cracker

Mr Theodore Dunnett of Oxford ran amok in his own house in 1972. He ripped the telephone from the wall, smashed to pieces a three-piece suite, threw a TV set and tape-deck into the street, kicked a wardrobe down the stairs, smashed windows and tore the bath from its plumbing. His explanation: 'I was shocked by the overcommercialization of Christmas.'

Driven to Worry

Ronald George of Stroud, in court to answer for various driving offences, excused himself thus: 'My mind was preoccupied with the thought of my grandson, who is in hospital with a broken thigh; my brother, who is seriously ill in another hospital; my wife, who is caring for my 80-year-old mother-in-law; and my sister, who has collapsed under the strain of looking after her – to say nothing of the stress involved in the reorganization of local government.'

Under the Influence

Charged with being 'drunk in charge of a pram', a proud father told the court. 'Wine makes me happy. I was pretending to be drunk to entertain my child.'

Pudding Pressure

A speeding food salesman in 1972 told his accusers that 'I was exceeding the speed limit because the hot black puddings in the car for delivery had steamed up the speedometer.'

Teething Problems

Arrested by Indiana Highway Patrol officers for driving dangerously slowly down the middle of an eight-lane interstate highway, a suspect motorist blithely reported: I was looking for my dentures, which had been thrown out of the window by accident when they became embedded in the wing of a chicken I was chewing.'

Emergency Mission

Fined £35 in 1974 for speeding through the Buckinghamshire town of Lechlade, travelling salesman Barry Winner paid up without demur, but had to explain: 'I forgot myself. But at the far end of the town they were screaming for toilet rolls.'

Duty Calls

Henri Chopin was arrested on Lorient Beach, Brittany, for appearing naked in contravention of local by-laws. M. Chopin sprang to his own defence. Others, he appreciated, might well have been illicit nudists, but 'I am not a nudist. I am a member of 'Decency', an anti-nudist group. I had been sent to the nudist colony as a spy.'

Unfortunately for the uncovered agent, the proximity of four nubile girl nudists had left him unable to maintain his composure. 'I was just asking my way off the beach', added M. Chopin, but the police still pounced.

Sick of Being Poor

Mr Patrick Dooley, of no fixed abode, admitted himself to Halifax Infirmary. Pausing only to organize a raffle and collect the subscriptions, he discharged himself. In his defence he claimed: 'It seemed a good way of getting some money.'

A Passing Shot

Accused of indecent exposure in Chorley, Lancashire, the defendant told the court: 'I was not standing naked at the window, but merely passing it on my way from the bathroom into the bedroom.' Asked why, then, his accuser, a local housewife, had seen him peeping around the window frame, he added, 'I had been looking for a mouse in the backyard. I had been intending to shoot it.'

Changing Colour

Hired as a Tory Party worker in a solid Labour seat, neophyte politico Simon Finson started off by reading the manifesto. This done, he told fellow workers: 'I'm just popping out for fifteen minutes.' Three hours later he returned to the constituency – as the new Liberal candidate.

Asked to explain this policy turn-around, he said, 'I know my chances are hopeless, but so are those of the Conservatives. When I read their manifesto I realized there was no real difference between us and them so, in order to give the public a fair chance, I decided to have a go.'

HIGH TECH

Science marches on unrelenting – encompassing the good, the bad and the technically abysmal.

Choked

Dr Dionysus Lardner (1793-1859), professor of natural philosophy and astronomy at University College, London: 'Rail travel at high speed is not possible because passengers, unable to breathe, would die of asphyxia.'

The good doctor also pooh-poohed the idea of transtlantic ships because 'they would require too much coal for their size.' A short time later the Great Western Railway had forced him to rethink his pronouncement.

Drug Crazed

Sigmund Freud, writing in his book *Uber Coca* (1884) on a white powder extracted from the coca leaf: 'Exhilaration and lasting euphora, which in no way differs from the normal euphoria of the healthy person . . . You perceive an increase in self control and possess more vitality and capacity for work. In other words, you are simply more normal, and it is soon hard to believe that you are under the influence of any drug.'

The powder was cocaine.

In 1898 an even more useful drug was synthesized – diacetylmorphine. First reports gave it a clean bill of health: 'a safe preparation free from addiction-forming properties'.

Typical was James R. L. Daly's anlaysis in the *Boston Medical and Surgical Journal* of 1900: 'It possesses many advantages over morphine . . . It is not hypnotic and there is no danger of acquiring the habit.'

The wonder drug was heroin.

Hot Air

In 1896, Lord Kelvin, perhaps the greatest scientist of his era, wrote: 'I have not the smallest molecule of faith in aerial navigation other than ballooning.'

In 1900 Mr Worby Beaumont, a leading engineer, was asked by a newspaper on the first day of the new century: 'Shall we fly?' Chuckled Beaumont: 'Yes, before the next hundred years have gone, in all likelihood. But the present generation will not, and no practical engineer would devote himself to the problem now.'

In 1901, Simon Newcomb (1835-1909) opined: 'Flight by machines heavier than air is unpractical and insignificant, if not utterly impossible.'

In 1903, the Wright brothers took off at Kitty Hawk.

Unacceptable

Ernst Mach (1836-1916), professor of physics at the University of Vienna: 'I can accept the theory of relativity as little as I can accept the existence of atoms and other such dogmas.'

Crossed Wires

In 1900 an article appeared in a London newspaper entitled 'Looking Ahead to the New Century'. It read: 'Probably Mr Marconi will succeed in signalling without wires to America from his laboratory at Poole, but the cable companies have no fears, for the rate of transmission in aetheric telegraphy is much slower than where wires are employed.'

Smashing Time

During the 1920s British scientists, under the leadership of Sir Ernest Rutherford, were busily engaged in bombarding atoms. The scientific community considered it an exercise in pure research, without any possible practical application, military or civilian. Indeed, Sir Ernest's long-standing toast at the annual Cavendish Laboratory dinner was: 'To the electron – may it never be of any use to anyone.'

Even when, in 1932, Sir Ernest and his team managed to split the atom, he remained unimpressed with its potential: 'The energy produced by the breaking down of the atom is a very poor kind of thing. Anyone who expects a source of power from the transformation of these atoms is talking moonshine.'

Roll On, R101

Lord Thomson of Cardington on the airship R101 in 1929: 'People are always asking me to give a name to R101. I hope it will make its reputation with that *name*.'

R101 duly made its name when it crashed at Beauvais one year later on its maiden flight.

Loony Tunes

In 1925 a *Daily Express* editor told a reporter, after being informed that a John Logie Baird was downstairs in reception: 'For God's sake go down to reception and get rid of a lunatic who's down there. He says he's got a machine for seeing by wireless! Watch him – he may have a razor on him.'

That same year Baird publicly demonstrated his invention, which he called television.

The Best is Yet To Come

J.B.S. Haldane, the Cambridge scientist, in 1937: 'I do not believe in the possibility of anything much worse than mustard gas being produced.'

Timely Warning

In 1972 TV cameraman George Brown, from Austin, Texas, received a letter from General Motors informing him that: 'We're recalling all 1972 Vega cars because of a defect that might cause the rear axle to disengage.'

George dutifully drove his Vega back to his local dealer. Four blocks away the rear axle fell off.

Red Spuds?

After twelve years of concentrated research, the Carlsberg Research Centre in Copenhagen announced in 1978 that it had finally succeeded in crossing a tomato with a potato plant, thus producing a 'pomato'. Said the head of the centre in making the announcement: 'We look upon the pomato as a major contribution to solving the world's food/population balance. When it is ready to enter the battle of our common agricultural needs, the fruit will combine the taste of the tomato with the nourishing power of the potato.'

Unfortunately, it turned out to also contain a deadly poison.

The Odd Couple

The war years in America saw an unlikely partnership between the flamboyant, fast-talking, eccentric West Coast shipbuilder extraordinaire, Henry J. Kaiser, and the reclusive, publicity-shy, equally eccentric West Coast movie producer cum oil tycoon, Howard Hughes. The object was to produce Kaiser's brainchild – a fleet of giant cargo planes – thereby winning the war with a few broad stokes. Explained Kaiser: 'The position of our enemies will be hopeless. We will be able to put down a vast army, anywhere in the world, within a single week. We will be free once and for all of the fear of having our armies cut off in some place distant from our shores . . . the whole world will be our front yard. And our enemies will be beaten to their knees.'

This was heady stuff, and although Washington was highly sceptical about backing the two ill-matched bedmates, popular opinion forced them into it. Kaiser, however, displayed a disturbing lack of technical knowledge about his subject. When a reporter had the temerity to ask him how cargo planes were built, Kaiser brushed him aside with: 'There's nothing to that. Our engineers have plans on their drawing boards for gigantic flying ships beyond anything Jules Verne could ever have imagined.'

The first design the team coughed up was truly a Jules Verne hallucination – a gigantic eight-engine, 200-ton wooden seaplane with a wingspan longer than a football pitch and a hull higher than a three-storey building. The monster appalled War Productions Board chairman Henry Nelson, but Hughes had powerful friends in Washington, notably the head of the Reconstruction Finance Corporation, Jesse Jones. When Nelson asked Jones's opinion of the people with whom he was dealing, Jones airily replied: 'You are safe in proceeding with Howard Hughes. I have known him since he was a boy – and I knew his father before him – and I know of no more capable and reliable man than Howard Hughes. Now, whatever you do, Henry, do not interfere with Howard. He is thorough and he is a genius and do not interfere with him.'

It was not until five years later – long after the war had been won – that the 'first' of Kaiser's 'fleet' was unveiled. Nicknamed the Spruce Goose, it was in fact a giant turkey. The largest aircraft ever constructed, it 'flew' just once – skimming the top of Long Beach harbour for about half a mile, with Hughes at the helm. After that it was trundled into a specially constructed hangar where it remained in mothballs at a cost of around a million dollars a year.

Flea Bitten

Henri Mignet, a French aeroplane enthusiast, lived a life inspired by a single dream – that everybody should be able to fly. To this end he designed his own packing-case aeroplane – the HM8 or Flying Flea as it became popularly known. Although an ugly tandem-winged, snub-nosed beast with a coffin-shaped fuselage and an outboard motor, the Flea was Mignet's pride and joy, and he burned to share his invention with the world. In a book outlining the Flea's unique specifications, he boasted: 'It is not necessary to have any techical knowledge to build an aeroplane . . . If you can nail together a packing case you can construct an aeroplane.' More than a thousand Frenchmen, Americans and Britons took him at his word, and the summer of 1935 saw a frenzy of back-yard Flea construction on two continents.

The *Daily Express*, quick to jump on the bandwagon, sponsored a visit by Mignet to show the British how to do it. Mignet made it to Calais, but crashed before setting out across the Channel. Although he made it the next day, it was only just, and from then on it was all downhill for the Flea.

The first British Flea ended its maiden voyage wrecked on its back in a cabbage patch. Most of those that followed failed even to lift off before crashing. Of those that did, a good number quickly flipped over onto their backs, a position from which it was impossible to shift them. After killing eleven pilots in France and Britain, the Flea's permit to fly was revoked. Uninjured by his many crashes, however, Mignet continued to experiment and build new versions of the Flea until his death in 1965.

Daddy Knows Best

Robert Oppenheimer, American physicist, on his brainchild the A-bomb, in 1946: 'I'm not sure that the miserable thing will work, nor that it can be gotten to the target except by oxcart. That we become committed to it as a way to save the country and the peace seems to me to be full of dangers.'

Slow to Learn

In 1920, the *New York Times* ridiculed Professor Robert Goddard, one of the fathers of space exploration, for his hair-brained assertion that rockets could function in a vacuum. Wrote the *Times* on January 13th: 'He seems only to lack the knowledge ladled out daily in high schools.' In July 1969, following the successful voyage of Apollo 11, the *Times* belatedly apologized.

Deep Water

Sir Richard Woolley, Astronomer Royal, in 1956: 'Space travel is utter bilge.'

The Bricklin

In 1974 a Philadelphia entrepreneur, 35-year-old Malcolm Bricklin, obtained $20,000,000 from the Government of New Brunswick, Canada. His plan: to create a super-sports car, adorned with all mod cons including a revolutionary fibre-glass acrylic body, gullwing doors, retractable headlights and the rest.

In September a prototype appeared, driven by Richard Hatfield, who was conveniently campaigning to retain his job as New Brunswick premier. *Playboy* magazine was chosen for a booster spread: covered with Bunny girls, the car was lauded indeed. 'The Bricklin has a gutsy, don't-tread-on-me look about it.'

The roadster's advertising campaign made the car's none-too-unique selling proposition very clear: 'Sooner or later you are going to drive a Bricklin. It might prove to be the first great sexual experience of your lifetime.' Prime Minister Hatfield told those who would listen: 'I have a gut feeling about this man.'

Alas, the Bricklin proved far from a turn-on. Quite the reverse. The doors wouldn't work – neither open, shut or lock correctly – and what customers there were were advised not to drive in the rain. The bodywork, made from a substance hitherto reserved for lavatory seats, proved useless for larger constructions, let alone moving ones.

Bits of the Bricklin also tended to fall off at speed. Not that there was much of that, anyway. Over 35mph it was noted that the shock absorbers fell off.

As for the hapless taxpayers who had backed the New Brunswick loan, the damned car wasn't even manufactured there. It was assembled locally, but parts came from Michigan and California. The Company's travel bills for a year topped $300,000. To finish things off, Bricklins cost around $6,300 per car to make, and the dealers were buying them for only $5,400.

The Bricklin died in prototype. The punters in New Brunswick, including women and kids, paid an average of $30 each to fund this automobile turkey. Spread across the whole of Canada the bill was 12 cents per head. Bricklin himself moved on, and the local paper obituarized the affair: 'So here you have one of the great promotional geniuses of our time, and what he lacks in business acumen, why he makes up in, ah, entrepreneurship. . .'

Clipped Wing

October 15, 1964, was a landmark day in the annals of US military development. On that day the Secretary of Defense, Robert McNamara, announced in Fort Worth, Texas, the inauguration of a revolutionary new aircraft – the F-111 swing-wing fighter-bomber: 'The plane is the greatest single step forward in combat aircraft in several decades.'

After that, it was the downhill all the way. The plane immediately developed 'technical trouble' with its revolutionary swing-wing, but the airforce pressed on undaunted. Said a Defense Department spokesman, reassuring Congress in September 1966: 'The F-111 will be superior in its class to any other tactical weapons system in the world.'

By 1967 the ill-starred machine was tumbling from the sky with alarming regularity. Still, in September that year, General G. P. Disosway, Commander of the Air Force's Tactical Air Command, had these soothing words: 'No matter what you read in the newspapers, the F-111 does fly. It's certainly the most advanced aircraft right now, I suspect, in the whole world.'

In October of that year another one crashed. Still the Air Force did not give up. Richard Nixon, speaking during the Presidential campaign in El Paso, Texas, on November 2, 1968: 'The F-111 in a Nixon Administration will be made into one of the foundations of our air supremacy.'

By this time eleven had crashed. Nevertheless . . . Major Thomas Wheeler Jnr, speaking in August 1969: 'The F-111 is a fantastic airplane. It not only does its thing . . . it does it better than any other airplane in the Air Force.'

By then thirteen had crashed. Then, in December 1970, the Senate Permanent Subcommittee on Investigations issued a report calling the F-111 programme 'a fiscal blunder of the worst magnitude'. Of the 500 planes to be built, fewer than 100 would 'come reasonably close' to performing as originally intended.

Only One Problem

The *International Herald Tribune* reported that the authors of a long-term study of contraceptive methods have come out strongly in favour of the diaphragm. According to the newspaper, the researchers had found that the diaphragm method contained: 'no material risks, other than pregnancy'.

Getting the Shakes

When the San Onofre nuclear power plant – situated only half a mile from a dormant geological fault in California – was opened, the US Atomic Energy Commission called it 'a monumental step forward in the use of nuclear power as a source of future energy'.

In October 1973, after an accident which almost caused a nuclear disaster, the plant was closed down.

A Waste of Money

In 1974 Henry Carpenter, local demolition officer, was boasting the marvellous potential of the Edmonton Incinerator. This monster was capable of recycling some 2000 tons of rubbish a day. In other words 'It should produce a quarter of a million tons of metal a year, plus £500,000 worth of heat to feed the National Grid, as well as 1600 tons of baled waste per eight hours . . . Inflation would vanish if everyone got involved in recycled waste.'

Further questioning revealed less appealing facts. Mr Carpenter admitted, 'Unfortunately the incinerator has failed to come up to expectations and is, in fact, losing us £1500 a week.'

Wankel

The Wankel non-piston engine was the great leap forward in car design of the late 1960s. Everyone said so. According to *Sports Illustrated* in 1969, 'The reciprocating piston engine is as dead as a dodo.'

General Motors announced: 'The Wankel will eventually dwarf such major post-war technological developments as xerography, the Polaroid camera and colour television.'

US News and World Report predicted in 1970, 'Now on the horizon, the possibility of a revolutionary type of engine to power Detroit's car of the future.'

The quick rise in the price of petrol put an end to the expensive-to-run Wankel. As Mazda, the engine's greatest proponent, ruefully admitted in its 1976 advertisement: 'The world has changed. So has Mazda.'

Bug-Eyed

The mail-order advertisement that was going to make Mr Sidney Long's fortune read thusly: 'Convert your dead, cold, black-and-white TV into a multi-coloured fantastic picture.'

In 1972, soon after the ad appeared, Mr Long of Worthing, Sussex, was visited by Consumer Protection Inspector Christopher Tinley, who had bought one of Mr Long's converters for £2. It turned out to be a sheet of polythene stained with orange, green and blue stripes.

As Mr Tinley later told magistrates: 'I settled down to enjoy my new colour reception and all I saw was a dentist with a blue head and an orange bottom.' Mr Long confessed that his device still had a few bugs, but was very effective with outdoor scenes. He was fined £200.

SNAFU

Few new entries in the arms race have received such effusive praise as that which greated the announcement of America's Sheridan Tank project in 1966. According to Col Paul A. Simpson, manager of the project, 'The Sheridan Weapons System, with the Shillegah (anti-tank missile), will provide the Army with a major advancement in tank-like weapons systems and a significant improvement in fire power.' Other Army experts predicted that the Sheridan would be 'the fastest, deadliest and most advanced armoured combat vehicle ever devised' and promised the Allies 'a decided edge over Soviet armour'.

And, for a while, it all seemed true. Indeed, so 'deadly' was the Sheridan that within months disturbing rumours were circulating that the tank was even shooting itself. Apparently, when the Sheridan commenced firing, 'premature explosions' would blow off its own gun turret.

Nevertheless, on the eve of the tank's first public tryout in 1967, Maj Gen Edward H. Burba, the Army's number one tank development officer, was confident enough to declare: 'I really don't know what the Russians have, but I'd like to place a bet for a month's pay that this is better.' Fortunately for the General, there were no takers. Within thirty minutes of the tank's starting its manoeuvreability tests, smoke began pouring out of the turret and its three-man crew was leaping for their lives, shouting for fire extinguishers. The demonstration was hurriedly cancelled.

The US Secretary of Defense, Robert McNamara, who earlier had promised – somewhat recklessly – that 'the major part of the US task in Vietnam can be completed by 1965', was undeterred. In January 1968 he told reporters: 'Although the cost of the programme has risen substantially above the original estimates, it is believed that the tank will meet or surpass nearly all of its performance objectives.' Such optimism was hardly borne out by events back at the project: the newly arrived, custom-built ammunition was discovered to be the wrong size – in other words, unfirable. There remained but one option, voiced by Col Merritte W. Ireland, commander of the test unit: 'It is a fine vehicle for Vietnam.'

Although still dogged by 'technical bugs', the Army kept insisting the Sheridan was battle worthy. A secret Pentagon report leaked to the press proved less sanguine. Of the 54 Sheridans serving in Vietnam, 15 had suffered major equipment failures, 25 had undergone engine replacement, there had been 125 electronic circuit failures, 41 weapon misfires, 140 ammunition ruptures and 'persistent failure of the recoil mechanism of the 152mm gun'. Undaunted, the Army shipped off 171 new Sheridans to Vietnam in July 1969, vowing that the tank's problems 'now are solved'.

The Sheridan lasted only six more months in Vietnam until the Pentagon finally decided that it constituted a hazard to the lives of its own combat troops. In March 1970, after ten years of development and over a billion dollars spent. 'the most advanced combat vehicle ever devised' was quietly scrapped.

Blown Out

Salomon de Daus, a 17th-century French scientist, took a discovery to Cardinal Richelieu, the country's leading statesman. Steam power, he explained, was the energy of the future. Richelieu was unimpressed. 'To listen to him you would fancy that with steam you could navigate ships, move carriages; in fact, there's no end to the miracles which, he insists upon it, could be performed.' So insistent was de Caus that Richelieu lost his patience and had the inventor locked away in a lunatic asylum.

Three Miles High

When America's Three Mile Island nuclear facility malfunctioned in April 1979, the problem was initially dismissed by Jack Herbein, a Vice-President of Consolidated Edison, who owned the plant, as: 'a normal aberration'.

Thence followed a flurry of misinformation. Don Curry, the company's chief public relations flack, informed reporters that: 'just a small amount' of radioactive water had leaked onto the reactor's floor. Only a 'small amount?' reporters asked a company engineer. 'Well, no . . . 50,000 gallons.' (Later and NRC official conceded that in fact 250,000 gallons had leaked, covering the floor to a depth of 'several feet'.)

The company then issued another soothing statement: 'There have been no recordings of any significant levels of radiation and none are expected outside the plant. The reactor is being cooled according to design by the reactor cooling system, and should be cooled by the end of the day.'

This statement had the desired effect. According to maintenance man William Metzger: 'I'm not afraid. I think these plants are safe.' Plant worker William Wilsbach said, 'Do you think I'd work here if I thought it was dangerous?' Secretary Margaret Duffy added: 'Much ado about nothing!'

A few hours later, a valve automatically opened as the water was being drained off, shooting a surge of highly radioactive gas into the air. Three mile Island was hastily evacuated.

If You Can't Lick 'Em

In May 1975 the World Health Organization announced that it was running down its anti-malaria campaign because in the organization's own words: 'Malaria has been licked.'

That afternoon the WHO Deputy General, Dr Tom Lambo, was rushed to a Geneva hospital suffering from malaria.

Can You Hear Me Coming?

Supersonic air travel had been an international dream for years when the US, the Soviet Union and a joint Anglo-French project were all launched in the 1960s. But one by one they fell away. The American SST (Supersonic Transport) went first because the costs were prohibitive.

In 1973 the Russians seemed on course with their TU 144, nicknamed 'Concordski'. Air Commander E. M. Donaldson, air correspondent of the *Daily Telegraph*, wrote: 'Russia's TU 144 supersonic airliner, drastically altered in design and now performing extremely well, is likely to win the race to get into airline service before the Concorde.'

Unfortunately, the TU 144 that went to that year's Paris Air Show fell out of the sky, killing all crew and passengers. So much for Russia.

Which left the English and the French with a plane that started off as Concord and, in 1967, gained a 'French' 'e' on the end. Wedgwood Benn, then Minister of Technology, explained: 'From now on the British Concorde will also be spelled with an 'e'. The letter 'e' stands for excellence.'

While Concorde lagged behind schedule and the costs, inflation-borne, soared as high as the test models, the makers remained optimistic. Henry Ziegler, of the French manufacturers, said in 1973: 'A first come, first served policy has been adopted for purchasers of Concorde.'

But the real problems began when the plane started flying. Environmentalists immediately protested its noisiness while the makers rushed to counter their claims. In June 1975 Henry Marking, of British Airways, claimed that objections were 'grossly exaggerated. The new engines are far quieter than the prototypes. People who live near the airports will hardly notice the aircraft.'

When the first 'commercial' Concorde flew out of Heathrow on its maiden flight ten days later, air noise expert Geoffrey Holmes said it would take 'thirty of the noisiest subsonic aircraft all taking off together' to equal Concorde's noise level. Four weeks later the same plane visited Melbourne where Australian expert, Dr John Goldberg and Louis Challis & Associates, reported that the plane was even noiser than the 1972 prototype.

This was no help, and hardly accorded with the views of a government scientific adviser, Sir James Lighthill, who in 1971 had typified the Concorde's sonic boom, as it passed through the sound barrier into supersonic speeds, as 'a very friendly boom, like a pair of gleeful handclaps'. Nevertheless even then some £35,000 had been paid out as compensation for damage caused by Concorde's test flights, and witnesses spoke of 'a twenty-five pounder gun going off in the next field' and 'flying bombs landing half a mile away'.

Concorde flies on today, over limited routes, forced out of direct flights by the noise problem unloved by most of the 'first come, first served buyers' and losing money, despite high fare costs, on every flight.

Deep Sixed

In 1960 the US Navy launched the *Thresher,* a $45-million submarine, 279 feet long, 4,300 tons in weight, and destined to spearhead a new generation of super-fast, super-silent and super-deep nuclear submarines. From 1960 to 1963 the *Thresher* underwent severe testing, although a large proportion of those years were spent in dry dock being overhauled.

On April 10, 1963, the *Thresher* was testing at 1000-foot depths in the North Atlantic's Wilkenson Deep. Escorting the sub was the USS *Skylark,* a ship whose rescue facilities extended only to 850 feet, some 150 feet short of the *Thresher's* operational level. At 9.12 am the *Skylark* was radioed from 1000 feet down. The *Thresher* was 'experiencing minor problem. . .' Then came the chilling 'exceeding test limit'.

No rescue was possible. Several months later Navy searchers retrieved the *Thresher's* remains. Divers talked of 'an underwater junkyard', and 129 men were lost in the disaster.

Power Drunk

In the mid-1880s the fledgling US oil industry was owned by one man – John D. Rockefeller – and sited in one place, Pennsylvania. It was beginning to seem that the wells were drying up. Although the optimistic spoke of the expansion westward, Rockfeller's brilliant assistant, John D. Archbold, saw no point in hanging around. He sold off his Standard Oil Stock, hoping to abandon the gravy train before it ground to a halt, and pooh-poohed any thoughts of new drilling.

'Are you crazy, man?' he asked a fellow businessman, 'I'll drink every gallon of oil produced west of the Missisippi.' Archbold had no sooner disposed of his stock when, in 1885, a new 'land of grease' was discovered in northwestern Ohio and eastern Indiana. Standard Oil stock rose to even more prosperous heights, and even though it wasn't quite west of the Mississippi, Archbold was probably a very sick man, whether from consuming oil or not.

TO PUT IT MILDLY

Wisdom after the event is always easiest. Hindsight gives the onlooker the most wonderful advantages. Yet even then, things can seem just a little off-centre. To put it mildly. . .

Fickle Finger of Fate

Senator Robert F. Kennedy, speaking in 1967: 'Who knows if any of us will be around in 1972. Existence is so fickle. Fate is so Fickle.'

Governor George Wallace, one year later: 'I suppose one day somebody might throw something other than rotten eggs at me.'

Here Come the Cavalry?

On June 25, 1876, General George Armstrong Custer, at the head of 700 officers and men of the US 7th Cavalry, looked down at the Sioux Indian encampment at the Little Big Horn and promised his eager troopers: 'Hold your horses, boys. There's plenty down there for us all.'

Fruit and Nut

'Reuben?' mused a fellow townsman, 'Well, he's surely an inquisitive sort of a guy.' He was referring to Reuben Tice, the local electrician in Monterey, California, whose real enthusiasms were for his spare-time inventions. Tice had had some success in inventing electrical under-floor heating as well as a device to chill cocktail glasses, and in November 1967 he embarked on his masterwork a machine to take the wrinkles out of prunes.

All was going well until one night the machine exploded and a ten-inch-long cylinder struck 68-year-old Tice on the head. His body was discovered across his workbench, surrounded by the shattered machine and half a pound of prunes. Alas, they were still wrinkled.

Don't Wait Up

Captain L.E.G. Oates, a member of Robert Scott's ill-fated Arctic expedition in March 1912, prior to leaving the communal tent and disappearing into the snow: 'I am just going outside and may be some time.'

Collectors' Corner

Nelson Bunker Hunt, Texas millionaire in the grand style, set about cornering the silver bullion market with his brother and a business syndicate in 1979. As they bought and bought, the price of silver, an increasingly rare commodity, soared from $6 per ounce in early 1979 to $50 per ounce in January 1980. To underline his pre-eminence, Hunt didn't merely make the paper purchases, he actually called for his silver to be brought to Texas where he simply stored it away. At its peak the Hunt syndicate has amassed 200 million ounces of the precious metal. Interviewed about his hoarding, Hunt asserted: 'I am not a speculator, I am a market squeezer. I am just an investor and holder in silver.'

In early 1980, however, a combination of rumours and Hunt mistakes tore the bottom out of silver. The Hunts lost an estimated one billion dollars on the deals.

The Wheels of Time

When, in 1968, Robert Waters of Chywoon Knoll, Cornwall, asked his friend Daniel Splint for the name of a good, reliable garage which would give his 1960 Wolseley car a 'minor, rust-prevention paint job', Mr Splint told him: 'Such establishments are like gold dust, but I have always used Thomas's of Camborne. They are slow but thorough.'

In 1974, six years and six solicitors' letters later, the Wolseley had yet to be returned from the garage. Mr Waters had also made more than 200 fruitless telephone calls demanding his car. When questioned about the delay, the proprietor, Mr Thomas, explained: 'I very much doubt if he is in his right mind. It was a complex restoration job, basically sentimental. Of course his car isn't ready yet. Nor can I promise anything for the spring.'

Food for Thought

On July 14, 1970, California Highway Patrol officers checked a crashed car near Salinas. They questioned the driver, Dean Stanley Baker, who confessed: 'Officers, I have a problem.' The bearded Baker then fished into the pocket of his jeans and produced a bunch of severed, bloody fingers. He then explained his 'problem'. Given a lift by a man in Yellowstone Park, he had shot him dead. Uninterested in robbery, Baker had then cut open the body, torn out the heart, and eaten it raw. The digits were a gruesome souvenir.

See How it Runs

Agatha Christie's whodunnit *The Mousetrap* opened on November 25, 1952. Said the author: 'It's a nice little play, it might run a year, eighteen months. . .' Anthony Huntley Gordon, the newly appointed Company Manager, grudgingly allowed: 'Well, at least we'll get our Christmas dinner out of it.' The play has now become the world's longest running show ever.

S'Marvellous

'Can't anybody here play this game?' asked 72-year-old Casey Stengel, veteran manager of the New York Mets baseball team, as his no-hopers plunged to a season record of 120 defeats in 1962, a record for the major leagues. Star of the losers was 'Marvellous' Marvin Throneberry, who declared ingenuously: 'Things keep happening to me.' Marv's fans, bedecked with T shirts inscribed 'Vram' (Marv backwards), loved his on-field errors, but their hero peaked when he turned up late for a celebratory post-season dinner given in his honour. He wandered in, couldn't find his seat and left to eat a solitary supper in the restaurant across the street.

Drop by Drop

Senator Zachariah Chandler of Michigan pondered the increasing tension between North and South in the America of 1861: 'A little blood-letting might be necessary. . .'

The US Civil War lasted from 1861-to 1865.

Caveat Emptor

In 1968 investors were offered the prospectus of a new company. 'Commodity Speculations Ltd', headed by one Arthur Henry Lawrence. £20,000 was subscribed in £1 shares before the City of London fraud squad moved in. It appeared that Lawrence was in reality Robert Jacobs who, as Michael Knowles, had already posed as the 'Mr Big' of a 1966 series of cut-price insurance frauds. Not that the punters had gone unwarned: boldly stated amidst the small print they could have read, 'This investment is not for those who must have complete security and a guaranteed return.'

Hot Tip

Travis T. Hipp, disc jockey on KFAT-FM radio station in Gilroy, California, on his bulk purchase in 1980 of three hundred LPs by the Jonestown People's Temple Choir: 'They're an honest collector's item. Certainly there won't be any more albums by this group.'

Underarm Odour

Six to win. The last man's in. The date is February 1981, the test match between Australia and New Zealand. With honour, pride and a good deal of hard cash at stake, Aussie Captain Greg Chappell told his younger brother Trevor to make sure the New Zealand batsmen didn't take the match. As the Australian commentator put it: 'I believe he's going to bowl underarm. This is maybe a little disappointing.'

Chappell's delivery, within the rules though far from the once-vaunted spirit of the game, duly saved the runs. It also led to a minor international incident. New Zealand Prime Minister Muldoon called the affair 'Disgusting!' His Australian counterpart Malcolm Fraser admitted 'a grave mistake', while irate New Zealanders demanded that the Australian ambassador be recalled after this 'act of shame'.

Mummy's Ruin

'Death will come on swift wings to those that disturb the sleep of the Pharoahs'. Thus runs the curse that threatened those who opened the three thousand-year-old tomb of the Egyptian boy-king Tutankhamun in Luxor in February 1923. The leader of the archaeological expedition, Lord Carnarvon, scorned the curse, just as he had two other warnings. One, from a mystic named Count Hamon, told him: 'Lord not to enter tomb. Disobey at peril. If ignored will suffer sickness. Death will claim him in Egypt.' The other, relayed through nightclub owner Mrs Kate Meyrick by the brother of the King Fuad of Egypt, underlined the problem: 'It is ill work. The dead must not be disturbed. Only evil can come of it. Those who desecrate the resting places of the ancient dead do so at their peril. You will see.' Carnarvon *did* worry slightly – he consulted two fortune-tellers, both of whom forecast an early death. Still, he refused to abandon the dig.

Two months after opening the tomb, in April 1923, Carnarvon awoke in his Cairo hotel room and remarked: 'I feel like hell.' By the time his son had arrived, he was unconscious. That night he died, and his death was attributed to a mosquito bite. It was noted as being in the same place as a blemish on Tutankhamun's mummified body. At the moment of Carnarvon's death, every light in Cairo went out. Until they went on again, the members of the expedition lit candles and prayed. A few days later another archaeologist died. American Arthur Mace had told his companions; 'I feel terribly tired.' He then fell into a coma and died before doctors could begin to diagnose his illness.

The deaths continued. The Hon Aubrey Herbert, who as Carnarvon's half-brother witnessed the tomb's opening, had remarked even then: 'Something dreadful is going to happen to our family.' On September 27, 1923, he too died mysteriously. George Gould, one of the Earl's close friends, rushed to Egypt on hearing of Carnarvon's death. He visited the tomb. A day later he had a high fever and was dead within twelve hours. Archibald Reid, the radiologist who X-rayed the mummy, died of apparent heart failure on his return to England. Carnarvon's secretary, the Hon Richard Bethell, died suddenly. Bethell's father Lord Westbury killed himself in 1930, jumping 60 feet from the roof of his St James's Court flat. British industrialist Joel Wool, an early visitor to the tomb, died soon afterwards of a mysterious fever. By 1930 only two of the original expedition were still alive.

Forty years later, in 1970, one of those survivors, 70-year-old Richard Adamson, appeared on TV to 'explode' the myth of the curse. It was his third attempt to challenge the Pharoahs. On the first occasion he had spoken out, his wife died within forty-eight hours; the second time, his son had broken his back in a plane crash. This time Adamson left the Norwich TV studios only for his cab to collide with a tractor, throwing him into the path of a passing lorry. He escaped death by inches but admitted to 'second thoughts' about the curse.

The Tutankhamun Exhibition of 1972 was organized by Dr Gamal Mehrez, of Cairo Museum's antiquities department. Even though his predecessor had died within hours of signing the contract to send the Pharoah's mask to London, Mehrez remained a sceptic. 'I more than anyone else in the world have been involved with the mummies of the Pharoahs.

Yet I am still alive. I am living proof that the tragedies associated with the Pharoahs are just coincidence. I don't believe in the curse for one moment.' On February 3, 1972, the golden mask was crated for despatch to London. That day Dr Mehrez dropped dead. Apparently the cause was cirulatory collapse.

Of the six RAF transport command crewmen who flew the mask to London, three suffered accidents or losses and two died, still relatively young, of heart attacks. Since then the deaths seem to have abated. But then so has interference with King Tutankhamun. In the meantime, for other optimists, the Curse rests.

Life is Full of Distractions

Jacqueline Bouvier Kennedy Onassis: 'I always wanted to be some kind of writer or newspaper reporter. But after college . . . I did other things.'

Bobby Socks

'At this point', announced the police constable, giving prosecution evidence in a 1974 assault trial, 'the defendant struck me.' The PC then used the Court Usher to demonstrate the restraining grip he had used to subdue his assailant. As he did so, the rapt court heard a loud crack. 'I may have torn his shirt, Sir', muttered an apologetic bobby. An X-ray revealed that in fact the usher's elbow had been fractured.

Egg-Otistical

On his deathbed, Mr Moyse of West Ealing told his wife and daughter who were in attendance: 'Make sure I keep paying my way, even after I'm gone.' His wife Joan showed great ingenuity in carrying out his request. Mr Moyse was cremated; his ashes were then ground up to a fine powder and placed for future use inside the family egg-timer.

Your Time is Up

In 1974 Mrs Edward Horne was watching from an Australian beach as her ten-year-old son Billy splashed among the waves.

When she noticed he had company, she yelled: 'There's a little fish back there, Billy, you'd better come in.' The 'little fish' was, in fact, a shark.

I Am A Camera

In April 1930 three paintings submitted to the annual Royal Academy exhibition in London had to be withdrawn when it was noticed that they were actually photographs lightly painted over. The artist, Reginald Eves, later to be appointed the first official artist of World War II in 1939, admitted: 'I was pressed for time. I did it purely to save time. It has now been brought home to me that I did a very foolish thing.'

You Don't Say

Trades Union Congress Statement on Economics, TUC Conference, 1956: 'People in the higher income groups have greater spending power than those with small incomes.'

Sub Standard

On Navy manoeuvres in 1977, a torpedo boat zeroed in on what its officers presumed was a regulation target. This was not so. Their salvo neatly demolished the Australian Navy's submarine, HMS *Oxley*. An apologetic Naval Information Officer announced later: 'It does show that we can hit what we were aiming for. We could have hit anything in the entire Pacific, but we actually hit what we were aiming at.'

Hail to the Lord

In November 1979, while crossing the House of Commons lobby, Lord Hailsham spotted his friend, Neil Marten MP, coming towards him. Remembering that it was Marten's birthday, Hailsham waved his hand and called out to him 'Neil!' Whereupon a gaggle of tourists, overcome by the grandeur of the Commons, all fell to their knees.

I Don't Like Mondays

Most parents welcome a little interest in their offspring from loving grandparents. Not so the mother of 15-year-old Edmund Emil Kemper, who was invited for a weekend in California with the old folks in August 1964. 'Don't bother', she told them. 'The boy's a real wierdo.' But they insisted, and Ed duly appeared. On August 27th, Ed picked up their phone to report on his holiday. It had not gone well. Standing with a still warm shotgun he told his Mom: I just wondered how it would feel to shoot grandma.' Kemper was jailed for five years.

In 1973 Ed made another call. It was to the local police department. 'I think I should give myself up', he announced, then catalogued a ghastly list of activities including sadism, cannibalism, murder, mutilation, necrophilia and allied excesses. In particular, he had used a hammer to back up his own hands when he killed off his mother and a visiting friend. Kemper continues to serve his life sentence.

Monkey Business

On day in 1974 a monkey appeared at the home of Amelia Roybal in Albuquerque, New Mexico. It came inside, went straight to the family medicine cabinet and consumed pills, hand lotion, eye drops and some cleaning fluid. It then unplugged the television, rampaged among the china cabinets, tossed valuables at its hosts and finished off by gulping down a bowl of plastic fruit. Said Ms Roybal, after the simian had been dispatched: 'He was very nice and gentle until he started drinking.'

With A Song in My Heart

In 1974, a 22-year-old Oregon disc jockey cued up another record for his easy-listening audience. It was 'Softly As I Leave You'. Then, as the record turned, the DJ hanged himself with the office telephone cord.

Crackers

In 1971 South Carolina legislator Woody Brooks barely escaped death when his State House office was flattened by packages stored on the floor above. Looking at the eight tons cf crackers which had been stockpiled in case of nuclear hostilities, Brooks remarked, 'Well, we knew there were *some* crackers back there.'

Cat's Paw

John Wiltshire, assistant manager of the Warragamba Lion Park in Australia, after his lion 'Fraulein' had savagely mauled an employee in 1974: 'Fraulein isn't a killer, just a playful stirrer.'

Say No More

Jeremy Thorpe, former leader of the Liberal party, quoted in *Behind the Image* by Susan Barnes, 1974: 'There are things that one passionately wants to keep private. Things that are no one's business. What isn't realized is how professionally I don't expose what I don't want to.'

Hairy Farce

Like many self-made millionaires, a certain Stateside entrepreneur fancied putting his cash into financing a little culture. He had met a theatrical manager at a party and been delighted when a suggestion was made that he back Eugene O'Neill's distinctly upmarket *The Hairy Ape*. The cash appeared, the manager hired a team, and the 'angel' duly vanished until curtain up. What he saw was theatrics, but not O'Neill. His funds had gone to putting on a saucy French farce. When he complained, the manager smiled. 'Hey, you know how these things always get changed around a bit in rehearsal. . .'

Unfair Cop

In 1964 Detective Sergeant Challenor, a member of the British Constabulary, was arrested by his men and charged with planting half-bricks on demonstrators before a visit by Queen Fredericka of Greece. Deploring the officer's fate, Home Secretary Henry Brooke announced sympathetically, 'His excessive devotion to duty appears to have precipitated a mental breakdown.' Later, Challenor was found to have been instrumental in framing twenty-six innocent people, thirteen of whom had been jailed.

Horizontal Hold-Up

Honchos at US detective agency Pinkertons were slightly worried about one of their employees, Ralph P. Distafano: 'He's efficient enough, but I guess the boy's been acting kinda kook-a-boo lately.' Or, as Distafano, the son of a cop and the brother of another, had put it just that week: 'The Jews in New York have got an electronic device in my head and are running me.'

On June 21, 1972, the 'kook-a-boo' gumshoe entered an employment agency in Cherry Hill, New Jersey. He was carrying a pair of 0.22 rifles. Seventy shots later, six men were dead and six more badly wounded. The seventy-first shot Distafano put through his own head.

You Said It. . .

Electioneering in 1976, Jimmy Carter promised, 'I don't pretend to know all the answers.' By 1980 he had proved at least this campaign statement true: only 20 per cent of Americans supported him, even fewer than Richard Nixon's disastrous 22 per cent on the eve of his resignation, making Carter the least popular supremo ever in the US.

I AM THE GREATEST

If you've got it, flaunt it. And if you haven't, wing it.

Lion-Hearted

One afternoon in 1969, weaving drunkenly among the other visitors at the San Francisco Zoo, was 59-year-old Amos Watson. Clutching a near-empty bottle of wine, he challenged the world: 'Come on you bastards, come on! Come and get me!' At this point Mr Watson fell into the moat surrounding the lion enclosure. Tommy, a five-year-old male, had obviously heard his challenge.

When the keepers managed to drag the tramp out of the moat, after shooting Tommy dead, Watson was rushed to hospital. Both legs were broken, as was his collarbone, and his body was slashed with deep cuts and bites. Despite all this, he lived to fight another day.

Mister Big

In November 1924 Dion 'Deanie' O'Bannion, altar boy turned safe-cracker and bootlegger, was looking to consolidate his power in gang-ridden Chicago. As boss of the Irish faction O'Bannion inevitably came up against the Italians, led by Al Capone. O'Bannion pushed his luck by setting up Capone's cousin Johnny Torrio for his first arrest. This irritated Capone, who issued threats, but Deanie was unimpressed: 'To hell with them Sicilians', he told the world.

A few days later, three customers entered O'Bannion's flower shop and asked about a wreath for another villain,

Mike Merlo, shot down that week. Before O'Bannion could answer, one man was holding his arm as the others pumped six slugs into him. Capone sent a $50,000 wreath to the late flower-seller's funeral.

Capone was never a good man to cross – or to befriend. Jake Lingle, a Chicago newspaperman, considered himself right in there with the mobs. One drunken lunchtime in the Capone speakeasy, Lingle boasted: 'I fix the price of beer in this town.'

His claim was quickly reported to Scarface Al. Lingle was shot down the same day.

Jack 'Legs' Diamond, a Capone gunman and alleged architect of the 1929 'St Valentine's Day Massacre', when George Moran's gang were butchered in a garage, was fond of saying: 'The bullet hasn't been made that can kill me.'

The obvious exception hit him in 1931 – fired, it is thought, by Moran himself, who had survived the massacre.

If Capone and Co ran America, those Mafiosi who hadn't bothered to emigrate kept on with business as usual in Sicily. In the small town of Corleone, a Mafia stronghold, there were 153 murders between 1944 and 1948. Two were those of the Grisi brothers. When one found his brother dead on a railway line, he vowed vengeance: 'The Mafia here are good for nothing but toothpicks!'

This opinion was duly reported to the local boss, Luciano Liggio. The second Grisi brother did not survive the night. He was shot down in public on Corleone's main street.

Never Say Die

Actor John Barrymore assured a companion during his final illness in 1942: 'Die? I should say not, old fellow. No Barrymore would allow such a conventional thing to happen to him.'

Lord Palmerston's last words, in 1865, were: 'Die, my dear doctor? That's the last thing I shall do.'

Handy Man

Quoted in Australia's *Bulletin* magazine in 1971, Sir Ralph Freeman, of leading architects Freeman, Fox & Partners, said: I'm very good with my hands, I can do anything with them.'

Sir Ralph had perhaps overlooked one aspect of his firm's recent efforts – the design of Melbourne's ill-fated Westgate Bridge. In Australia's greatest bridge disaster, thirty-eight of the sixty-five workers on the box-girder construction had died during its erection when a section plunged 160 feet into the Yarra River on October 15 1970. Overall losses were estimated at $10 million.

If I Ruled the World

Nicholas Fouquet, finance minister to King Louis XIV of France, added to his coat of arms a Latin inscription which, in translation, read: 'How high can I not rise?'

This rhetorical question was answered soon afterwards when Fouquet entertained the king at his own château. So appalled was Louis by his minister's opulence, obvious wealth and thus threatening power that he had Fouquet arrested, charged with embezzlement and jailed. He died in prison.

I Mean What I Say

Eugene 'Bull' Connor, police commissioner of Birmingham, Alabama, in 1950: 'I ain't gonna let no darkies and white folks segregate together in this town.'

The Sky's the Limit

Barry Goldwater, US senator and former presidential candidate, said after Apollo XI's successful flight in 1969: 'Since America landed two men on the moon, there is no problem we cannot solve.'

Winning Isn't Everything

Harold Wilson, British Prime Minister, prior to losing the 1970 election: 'If I were a football manager, on present form I would be more worried about job security than I am as Prime Minister.'

Lost and Found

Jimmy Hoffa, the former head of the American Teamsters' Union, was released from jail in 1975. That year he told *Playboy* magazine, when asked about his future: 'It's survival of the fittest, my friend.'

Later he told interviewers, 'Everybody knows where I am. I have never had any bodyguards and I always drive myself. If anyone wants to get me, they know where I am.'

So they did. Hoffa vanished, presumed murdered, on July 30, 1975.

Confidence Counts

The Shah of Iran, 1978: 'Nobody can overthrow me.'

Senator Edward Kennedy, April 15, 1980: 'I can win both the nomination and the presidential contest.'

Luck of the Irish

Flushed with the success of his big hits of 1966 – 'You Were On My Mind', which reached No. 2 and lasted fourteen weeks in the top thirty, and 'Pied Piper', up to No. 5 and thirteen weeks in the charts – Irish singer Crispian St Peters announced: 'I'm going to be bigger than the Beatles.'

Mr St Peters released one more song that year, called 'Changes'. It managed four weeks of popularity, rising no higher than No. 47 in the charts. And that, it would appear, was that.

Shooting Match

TV mogul, talk show host and American media star David Susskind was as keen on the Gary Gilmore story as the next hustler. Prior to bidding for the rights of the story of America's first execution in over a decade, Susskind dismissed his major rival, Larry 'Hell's Agent' Schiller – a worthy opponent who had already done posthumous tales on Lenny Bruce, Marilyn Monroe and others – with: 'Any contest between me and Mr Schiller would be like the Dallas Cowboys playing the local high school.'

It must have been off-season for the Cowboys. Susskind's slicker style alienated Gilmore's family, and Schiller divided an alleged $1 million with author Norman Mailer for the best-selling *Executioner's Song*.

Way to Go

Bob Fitzsimmons, an English prize fighter, was matched in 1902 against the American champ Jim Jeffries, a 6 foot 2 inch, 220-pound pug. He commented, 'The bigger they are, the harder they fall.'

A right to the belly, a left hook to the jaw, and Fitzsimmons left the ring, carried out feet first.

Sonny Liston, heavyweight champ, said prior to facing the cocky young Cassius Clay in 1963: 'If they ever let me in the ring with him, I'm liable to get put away for murder.'

In the fight on February 25, 1964, Liston failed to come out of his corner for the seventh round. He claimed, nonetheless, to have been unimpressed by Clay. 'He won't be staying champion for too long.'

On May 25, 1965, Clay (now Muhammad Ali) knocked Liston out after 1 minute and 42 seconds of the first round.

I Am the Greatest

Ali himself, the 'Louisville Lip' as early fans and critics nicknamed him, was never exactly subdued. 'I am the greatest!' he told the world, and in 1963, looking to the future, said: 'I figure I'll be champ for about ten years, then

I'll let my brother take over – like the Kennedys down in Washington.'

Later, unconscious of the awful irony of *that* phrase, Ali boasted: 'The man who will whip me will be fast, strong, and hasn't yet been born.' Other, that is, than Joe Frazier, Larry Holmes, Ken Norton and Leon Spinks.

Beating Ali, of course, was a special triumph in itself. The normally quiet Joe Frazier, envisioning the rematch with Ali, whose jaw he had already broken, told *Playboy* in March 1973: 'You ever get a kid when you talk to him and play with him, he don't wanna stop and you gotta whip his ass to make him behave? That's what this monkey Clay is like.'

Frazier duly lost his rematch, and the Ali saga, a succession of rescinded retirements, continues.

I Am the Champion

Bobby Fischer, the reclusive, idiosyncratic American chess champion, said in 1961: 'I'm going to win the world championship, hold it a couple of years, and then take up something else and make a lot of money.'

The first part, yes; the second. . .

Soccer star George Best, reminiscing ruefully in 1974 about the golden dreams of a Belfast teenager: 'Once I started playing football I realized I was in the perfect position for pulling birds. I had the limelight, the publicity, the money. Where could I go wrong?'

Superstuntman Evel Knievel, prior to his Snake River Canyon jump in 1974: 'Before the jump I'm going to have the biggest party you ever saw at the Freeway Tavern in Butte. I'm going to drop one million dollars. I'm inviting Liz Taylor, the Pope, whatever the Greek husband of Jackie Kennedy calls himself and the entire city of San Francisco. If you think Jesus had a Last Supper, wait till you see mine!'

On the night, Knievel managed to drag a few cronies on a brief tour of Butte's bars. On the day, the jump turned out to be no great shakes either. He crashed halfway through the jump, although his parachute opened as soon as he left the ramp in anticipation.

Women's Work

In 1973 tennis hustler Bobby Riggs, a 55-year-old former star, challenged and defeated the current women's number one, Margaret Court. She went down 6-2, 6-1. Riggs crowed and used the whipping to abuse the burgeoning Women's Movement. Billy Jean King, a feminist as well as a top player, forthwith challenged the cocky Riggs. He sneered: 'She's a great player, for a gal. But no woman can beat a male player who knows what he's doing. I'm not only interested in glory for my sex, but I want to see Women's Lib back twenty years, to get women back in the home where they belong.'

On September 20, 1973, Billy Jean destroyed Riggs in three straight sets, 6-4, 6-3, 6-3, in front of thousands who packed the Houston Astrodome and millions who watched a thirty-six nation telecast. Afterwards Billy Jean leaped the net, threw an arm round her opponent and soothed 'Good try, Bobby'.

Ari-vederci

During the late 1950s those sufficiently interested to look up from the green baize tables could have witnessed an all-out struggle for control of the luxury resort of Monaco. On one side was the ruler, Prince Rainier; up against him was the Greek Shipowner Aristotle Onassis. Their clash was centred on the shares of the Societé de Bains de Mer, the SBM, which effectively owned and ran Monaco's capital, Monte Carlo. In short, Rainier wanted to modernize the principality, and Onassis wanted to keep it quaint. Each had the power to frustrate the other. As the largest shareholder in SBM,

Onassis could control votes; as monarch, Rainier had the right of veto.

In 1959 the struggle intensified. SBM shares, until then a steady 1700Fr on the Paris Bourse, leapt in one month to 4200Fr. Rumours abounded until Onassis revealed that a company 'in which I am interested' had purchased 500,000 SBM shares, making him not only the largest single but the outright majority shareholder. As he happily informed Louis Vuidet, maitre-d' of the Hotel de Paris: 'I am the boss here now.'

But not for long. Rainier pondered, then struck back. 'The only solution', he announced, 'appears to be a test of force.' Using his royal prerogative, he had the state create 600,000 *new* shares. *He* was now the majority shareholder. Crushed and mortified, Onassis capitulated. He sold Rainier his own shares at rock-bottom prices and left Monaco.

SAVAGE IRONY

According to the UN Declaration of Human Rights (1948), 'All human beings are born free and equal in dignity and rights.' It sounds good at the time, but later. . .

On The Rocks

In 1907, sea captain E. J. Smith was interviewed on his lifetime spent at sea. The Captain answered modestly: 'When anyone asks me how best I can describe my experience in nearly forty years at sea, I merely say, uneventful . . . I have never been in any accident of any sort worth speaking about . . . nor was I ever in any predicament that threatened to end in disaster of any sort. You see, I am not very good material for a story.'

Four years later he was given command of the *Titanic* which, as everybody knew, was unsinkable.

The Shipbuilder magazine in 1911 thought it was the marvel of the age: The Captain may, by simply moving an electric switch, instantly close the doors throughout and make the vessel practically unsinkable.'

After the launching, reporters quizzed a deckhand busily engaged in loading luggage. Commented the worthy mariner: 'God Himself could not sink this ship.'

In 1912, on the eve of the *Titanic's* maiden voyage, the London *Evening Standard* reported: 'In the fight during the coming season, there will be a scent of battle all the way from

New York to the shores of this country – a contest of sea giants in which the *Titanic* will doubtless take high honours.'

Whereupon the *Titanic* steamed off over the horizon and hit an iceberg. Soon after the collision Major Peuchen, a yachtsman who would survive the sinking, remarked on a slight tilt in the deck. Replied his friend: 'Oh, I don't know. You cannot sink this boat.'

The first the world knew of the disaster was from the White Star Line's telegram to the press and relatives of those aboard: 'All *Titanic* Passengers Safe. The *Viginian* Towing the Liner into Halifax.'

On April 15, 1912, the New York *Sun* therefore duly reported: 'All Saved From *Titanic* After Collision'.

In fact, the *Virginian* was nowhere near the scene, and the *Titanic* was at the bottom of the ocean, along with 1,513 of its 2,300 passengers.

Watertight Reasoning

During the US Senate inquiry into the sinking of the *Titanic*, committee chairman William A. Smith distinguished himself by asking: 'Why didn't the passengers on the boat go into the watertight compartments and save themselves from drowning?' It was gently pointed out to him that the watertight compartments went to the bottom along with the rest of the *Titanic*. He became known as 'Watertight Smith' thereafter.

Just a Game?

In 1942, in the interests of fraternal relations, the German authorities in occupied Kiev instigated a series of soccer matches between victors and vanquished. Pronounced the Germans: 'We have nothing against sports. In fact, the opposite.'

Whereupon a crack team of German troops turned out against the local Kiev players and were promptly beaten 6-0. The nonplussed Germans retired to regroup before the next kickoff. This time they were beaten 5-1. The German authorities, more than a little irked, quietly took the Kiev players aside and warned that if there was a repetition of the previous outcomes, there would be trouble. The third-and last-match ended: Kiev 8, Germans 0. At the final whistle the Kiev team was marched off the pitch, taken away and shot dead.

How Could You?

Witch-hunting American Senator Joseph McCarthy, hoist by his own petard in 1956: 'I think it is a shoddy, unusual thing to do to use the floor of the Senate to attack your opponent without any proof whatever.'

Knock Knock

At about 8.30 pm on June 7, 1971, Kenyon F. Ballew of Silver Spring, Maryland, was reclining in his bathtub. His wife, dressed only in her underwear, was in the next room getting ready for bed. Suddenly there was uproar outside in the corridor, the apartment door burst open, and in rushed six wild-eyed, bearded men brandishing pistols and carrying an 85-pound battering ram.

Convinced that they were under attack by drug-crazed hippies, Mrs Ballew screamed for her husband to get a gun and, given that Mr Ballew was an avid gun collector, this was no empty threat. The Ballew apartment was crammed with firearms: nine cap-and-ball replica revolvers, three flintlock pistols, two cap-and-ball rifles, a 0.22 calibre semi-automatic pistol, an M-1 carbine, two 0.22 rifles, a 20-gauge over-and-under shotgun, a 12-gauge pump shotgun, a 12-gauge double-barrel shotgun and a military rifle with attached bayonet.

But, before Mr Ballew could squeeze off a shot, he was paralyzed by a bullet which ploughed into his forehead and through the left lobe of his brain. His wife, by this time almost demented by terror, screamed: 'Murder! Get the police! Police! Police!'

At this point the raiders lowered their guns, turned towards her, and said as one man: 'We *are* the police.'

Immortality Starts Here

Charged with clinical malpractice over his rejuvenation treatment, a Belgian physician claimed in court that, as his own chief guinea pig, he was certain to live 'for at least 1000 years'. The court remained unconvinced, and sentenced him to eighteen months' imprisonment, whereupon the doctor suffered a heart attack in the dock and was carried unconscious to a nearby hospital.

Night of the Long Knives

The wife of a St Alban's social worker awoke one night to hear her husband beside her, shouting in the dark: 'We are being attacked – I will protect you!' The terrified woman switched on the light and found she was covered in her own blood. Later, her husband told magistrates that he had dreamed he was being chased by a gang of football hooligans and has lashed out at them in his sleep. When he awoke he found he was stabbing his wife with a kitchen knife. He was acquitted.

Football Mad

M. Trichard, a Lyons bourgeois, was peacefully watching the 1978 soccer World Cup, then in its second week. That his own team, France, had long since been knocked out did not matter. He had watched every match. Thus when his wife asked him to shell the peas, he ignored her request.

'I am watching the football. Don't bother me.' He turned back to his television. Madame Trichard then removed the family shotgun from the wall and terminated her husband's soccer enthusiasm for ever.

His Master's Voice

Pat Nixon, 1973: 'Nobody could sleep with Dick. He wakes up during the night and switches on the light and speaks into his tape-recorder. It's impossible!'

Babs & David & Derry & Toms & Marks & Spencer. . .

In May 1973, Barbara Hulanicki's enormously successful London boutique Biba moved into the huge art deco Kensington department store, Derry and Toms. On the celebratory opening night, a Biba acolyte remarked facetiously to Hulanicki's husband David FitzSimon: 'Wouldn't this make a perfect site for a branch of Marks and Spencer's!'

FitzSimon chuckled along with the rest. Less than two years later, after losing £4.6 million, Biba gave way to Marks and Spencer.

Bum Deal

Scandalized by the soaring price of meat, Sacramento California lion-tamer Bianco Zamperia complained in 1974: 'I haven't been able to feed my lions anything but chicken – they like beef.'

Especially rump, so it would seem. During a performance shortly afterwards, one of his lions took a bite out of Bianco's buttock.

'Don't Drink and Drive'

It was Transport Minister Ernest Marples who coined the memorable safety slogan. He was banned in 1974 for driving under the influence of alcohol.

Bumper Bundle

When a young lady driving a mini-bus bearing the bumper sticker 'Honk If You Love Jesus' saw a car barrelling towards her with its horn blaring, she waved gaily. Seconds later there was a massive (albeit injury-free) crash. Apparently the other driver was not so much pro-Christ as brakeless.

In Houston in 1976 a female driver was seen sporting the mildly humorous bumper sticker: 'Don't Follow Me, I'm Lost!'

This became downright hilarious when she managed to mistake the double doors of a ship's loading bay for a garage exit and drove blithely into the oily waters beyond.

Off Side

Don Revie, the former England soccer manager, in 1977. 'Football in the 1970s is very rewarding financially and can provide the opportunity to travel to almost any country in the world.'

Revie quit the national team soon after and, to much scorn from his former colleagues, took on the lucrative task of managing in Saudi Arabia.

The Ones That Got Away

'30,000 pounds – It's a record!' radioed the captain of a Nova Scotia trawler after he and his crew had landed their best catch of the 1976 season. Unfortunately the boat's capacity was only 15,000 pounds. It sank.

Hedging Their Bets

Cyril Stein, Chairman of the bookmaking chain Ladbrokes, in 1978: 'It's not true that the bookmaker always wins.'

Too true. In 1979 Ladbrokes lost their casino licence and all their casinos in the face of allegations of corruption.

Second Coming

David Raiment, a 35-year-old building inspector, was perhaps not too nimble on his toes, but at least his timing was impeccable. Taking a short-cut home following an all-night party, Raiment found himself on top of the Claymore Memorial Church. Then, as the organ struck up 'Riches Shall Fall from Heaven on High, the roof gave way and crashed onto the heads of the congregation. Raiment later denied he was stealing lead from the church.

Home to Thee

Three of East Africa's leading evangelists worked as a trio and billed themselves as 'God's Favourite Children'. It was hard to tell whether this name was ironic or prophetic when the Almighty snatched them all to his bosom at once when lightning struck during a service at Oyo, Nigeria.

Lifeline

In 1978 the US Army in Germany wowed the locals with a tattoo entitled 'Patriotism is Life'. The centrepiece of the show was Sergeant George McGraw, whose parachute descent brandishing the Stars and Stripes was to climax the event. However, much of the effect was ruined when his parachute lines became entangled in Old Glory and he plunged to his demise in a convenient cemetery.

Safety First

Enthusiastic members of an Australian Safety Committee arranged a massive 2000-mile 'Push' from Hobart to Perth in 1978. A squad of nurses volunteered to push a hospital bed across the lengthy trek. 'We want to prevent careless accidents', the group explained. Unfortunately, somewhere along the route a member of the team fell beneath the rolling bed, and its castors broke her neck.

The Beauty of Modern Appliances

'I thought it was time to give Beauty's cage a good clean', explained a Durham housewife in 1972. Unfortunately for Beauty, a pet canary, her owner chose a vacuum cleaner to do the job. Mourning the late Beauty, she explained: 'I switched it on and . . . whoosh! One minute Beauty was chirruping away and the next all I could see was a tuft sticking out of the nozzle.'

It's All in the Mind

Allie MacLeod, manager of the 1978 Scottish World Cup soccer team: If the manager keeps saying, ''We'll win it, we'll win it, we'll win it'', eventually they believe you.'

He said it and they believed it, but that didn't seem to make a lot of difference to the result.

Leave of Absence

The Shah of Iran, in January 1979: 'I should like very much to take a vacation.'

The Ayatollah had the same idea in mind.

Tired And Emotional

After an 'exhausting' all-night party, Mr Tim Heywood and his girlfriend, Miss Janey Coke, were motoring home through the Norfolk countryside when Mr Heywood fell asleep at the wheel. The car, out of control, rocketed down a steep incline, clipped a pylon and ricochetted into a steel barrier before crashing into a retaining wall. Mr Heywood and his girlfriend staggered from the wreckage dazed but miraculously undamaged. Exclaimed Miss Coke, surveying the crumpled remains of the vehicle, whose engine had been reduced to less than a foot in length: 'Thank God we weren't hurt!' Mr Heywood, incensed by the loss of his sports car, angrily slammed the door – and chopped off his finger.

WHAT, ME WORRY?

Ignorance is bliss. For a while anyway. But what rude awakenings await the blithe. . .

Motorway Madness

In 1978 Australian conservationists were fighting doggedly against the construction of a proposed new motorway near Melbourne. One young demonstrator, interviewed by the local press, confessed that much of the demonstrating was really quite enjoyable: 'We have a good time. A lot of people come down to talk to us. Sometimes we get drunk and sing.'

Two hours later his arm was broken and several of his front teeth were knocked out in a police baton charge.

Resting Times Ahead

Former British Prime Minister Ramsay MacDonald was setting out for a South American cruise with his daughter Sheila on November 4, 1937. The press naturally requested his future plans. MacDonald told them simply: 'I have no plans. I am in search of that most elusive of all forms of happiness – rest.'

Five days later MacDonald died at sea.

Who, Me?

Lord Mountbatten of Burma, questioned in 1978 by some who feared that as a major national figure he might also find himself a No. 1 target for IRA terrorists: 'What would they want with an old man like me?'

Bad Breath

In 1974 a man was brought into the police station in Franklin, Tennessee, charged with being drunk and disorderly. He vehemently denied the charges claiming: 'I am sober. It's just my breath. Other people have had this impression. Whatever I eat, my breath smells of liquor.'

The officers were almost convinced – until their prisoner smiled winningly and fell unconscious from his chair.

Miner Disturbances

Prime Minister Edward Heath said, in a speech in November 1973: 'Our only problem at the moment is the problem of success.' Within four months Heath was in opposition, after 'the winter of Discontent', 'the Three-day Week', major strikes, power cuts and other Government-wrecking 'problems'.

The Sunshine Boys

During a tour of Santiago in 1981, KC, lead singer of the pop group KC and the Sunshine Band, was in trouble with the police following an incident with a journalist. The previous day the journalist, Franz Alida, had written in his column. 'KC is a liberated man, therefore he will not mind that I tell you this.'

Alida then went on to write that the burly KC was in fact bi-sexual and having an affair with a local newscaster. Next day, KC spotted Alida hanging around his hotel door along with other journalists, whereupon he and the rest of the band stormed out, threw Alida to the ground and, as one eye-witness alleged, 'put the boot in'. Alida was taken to hospital suffering two black eyes and a broken rib.

Inclement

In November 1951 Rudolf Slansky was Deputy Premier of Czechoslovakia and General Secretary of the Communist Party. The second most powerful man in the country, he was understandably surprised when State Security officials appeared at his home in the early hours of one morning to arrest him, along with his wife and son. Waiting in prison, he realized that his arrest had been on the express orders of Klement Gottwald, Czechoslovakia's President. With this in mind, his son Rudi tried to comfort his mother: 'I know it's hard Mummy, but if Comrade Gottwald knows of it, then Stalin must know and surely we can trust him.'

Young Slansky may have mused on this in later years. His father starred in the last and greatest of Stalin's show trials before going to his execution, and Rudi and his mother were formally disgraced and exiled.

Unprincipled

Addison Mizner, brother of the outrageous Wilson and architect extra-ordinaire of the fabulous Florida Land Boom of 1924, assured an old friend, Phil Boyer, that while the more foolhardy might speculate, *he* was OK: 'Don't you worry about me, Phil. I have a million dollars put away in Government Bonds, and you can rest assured that I'll never touch a penny of the principal.'

When the Florida property bubble burst soon afterwards, Mizner found himself utterly broke. He wound up running a nightclub in Los Angeles.

Lend Me Your Ears

Mr David Bleakley, Minister of Community Relations in Northern Ireland, was addressing the annual meeting of the Ulster Institute of the Deaf in 1972: 'I have never been prouder to be a citizen of Belfast than at this time. Protestant and Catholic, rich and poor, are maintaining a standard of community stability that compares with anything that has ever been recorded in the annals of Europe.'

The rest of Mr Bleakley's speech was punctuated by three explosions in the car park across the hall in which he was speaking.

Hair Razing

When he was sacked by the Philadelphia Fire Department, William Michini of Camden, New Jersey, sued for wrongful dismissal. Addressing the court in his own defence, he stated: 'To suggest that having long hair lessened my efficiency as a fire-fighter is madness. Before my hair reached the middle of my back, I was a weakling. Now my image has improved. I want to identify with the people whose houses I am saving from the flames. I am keen. Several doctors have told me that long hair helps a man become a good citizen. It is known as the Sampson Syndrome. To prove that long hair is not dangerous, that it is, in fact, self-extinguishing, I am going to conduct a small experiment.'

At this point, Mr Michini produced a Zippo lighter and set fire to the ends of his hair. The entire luxuriant growth was consumed in flames. But despite his tonsure, the Philadelphia Fire Department did not rehire Mr Michini.

Dead Drunk

On December 13, 1951, gangster Willie Moretti was summoned to appear before the Kefauver Committee investigating organized crime to testify as to his experiences of Mafia operations in New Jersey. True to the code of 'omerta' (silence), Willie told them simply: 'Nix'. After the hearing Willie got talking to George White, a Federal Narcotics agent who suggested they have a few drinks. In the resulting alcoholic haze, Willie turned somewhat more forthright. Yes, he agreed, there was a Maf. Yes, he was in it, but really, they weren't such bad guys. After all, they don't hurt anybody except each other. White agreed, but couldn't help saying that any gunplay at all had its drawbacks. Willie was indignant: 'Nothing like that happens any more unless someone is out of line. That's why Charlie (Charles 'Lucky' Luciano) is respected so much today. He got the fellows together and showed that it was bad business to go around shooting people.'

Unfortunately, Willie's little confession reached Luciano's ears. And Willie, it transpired, had been 'out of line'. Two months later he was executed, shot dead in a tavern in Palisades, New Jersey.

The Last Chord

Mozart was commissioned to compose his 'Requiem' in 1791. Aged only thirty-five and living parsimoniously on the remains of a once substantial fortune, working too hard and eating too little, Mozart was convinced that another composer was trying to poison him. Starting the 'Requiem', he prophesied: 'I am certain that I am writing a 'Requiem' for my own funeral.'

In fact, he died that year. His wife arranged the cheapest possible funeral, and then did not attend, put off by a rainstorm. The great composer's body was tossed into a mass grave as another anonymous pauper.

With Friends Like These

General George Armstrong Custer, six years prior to his arrival at the Little Big Horn, in 1870: 'The Army is the Indian's best friend.'

FAMOUS LAST WORDS

If you gotta go, then go. But say something, even if it's only goodbye.

No Laughing Matter

Sometime prior to the birth of Christ one Calchas, a Greek, was told by a seer that on a specific day he was destined to die of laughter. As the day in question drew to a close and Calchas found himself still hale and hearty, he remarked: 'There, I am not dead.' So amusing did he find this concept that he burst into laughter and died, laughing.

All In Fun

Brothel-keeper Jim Averill couldn't believe what his erstwhile clients were doing as they adjusted a noose round his neck one afternoon in 1888. Even as they kicked away the stool on which he stood, Averill remonstrated with them, 'Stop your fooling, boys!'

Massacre of the Innocents

For years Henry Plummer had run the Western town of Bannock, Washington, as a personal fief. Regularly re-elected sheriff, Plummer (who had already gutted Lewiston, Idaho) used his own gang to terrorize Bannock for personal gain. His boys were known as 'The Innocents', a sarcastic description of their ability to avoid any prosecution, and they numbered two hundred strong. Finally. Bannock's citizens banded together as vigilantes and captured some 'Innocents' who provided enough damning information to enable them to arrest the sheriff.

On January 10, 1864, Plummer and two dozen of his men were strung up on gallows originally erected as part of an 'Anti-Crime' campaign that Plummer had never implemented. As the noose was adjusted around his neck, an incredulous Plummer exclaimed: 'Boys, boys, you wouldn't hang your sheriff, would you?'

They did.

Nose for Trouble

A drunken customer in a Dublin coffeehouse in 1770 lurched against a fellow drinker. With the arrogance of the occupying English, he exclaimed: 'I smell an Irishman!'

To which his butt, an aristocrat and well-known duellist, replied, 'You'll never smell another!' drawing his sword, he promptly cut off the drunk's nose.

The Miller's Tale

On December 15, 1944, bandleader Glenn Miller, fresh from entertaining troops in Britain, was ready to move on to Paris. It was a cold, foggy day, and Miller was slightly dubious about the trip. An eyewitness who saw him climb into the plane heard an exclamation: 'Hey, where are the parachutes?' However, his objections were quickly overruled by his pilot, USAF Major Norman Basell, who shouted back to the worried bandleader: 'What's the matter, Miller? D'you want to live forever?'

With that, the plane lumbered into the air, but it never arrived in Paris. No corpses were ever found, nor was any wreckage ever retrieved.

No Worries

President Park of South Korea was having dinner when alleged members of the Korean CIA appeared to shoot him down. Two women tried to help him, one of them bending to ask: 'Are you all right, your Excellency?'

Park looked up: 'I am all right.'

Those were his last words.

Soldier's Farewell

On April 21, 1918, Rittmeister Manfred Freiherr von Richtofen signed a fan's autograph book and climed into his maroon Fokker Triplane. Von Richtofen, known as the 'Red Baron', was the leading Great War German air ace, with eighty kills to his credit. He mocked the autograph hunter's enthusiasm: 'Don't you think I'll come back?'

Later that day von Richthofen met his match in a dogfight with the Sopwith Camel piloted by Captain Arthur Roy Brown of 209 Squadron, RFC. The Red Baron did not survive the crash.

Apart from That, Mrs Kennedy. . .

On the morning of November 22, 1963, the day John F. Kennedy visited Dallas, Texas, the London *Daily Express* ran a photo of his Republican rival, Barry Goldwater. The caption read: 'The Man Who Is Gunning For Kennedy'.

On arriving in Dallas, Kennedy was driven from the airport. His companion in the official car was Mrs John Connally, wife of the then Governor of Texas. Turning to her Presidential guest, she indicated the cheering throngs and remarked: 'Well, Mr President, you can't say that the people of Dallas haven't given you a nice welcome'.

Hand-Out

Local people in the Buckinghamshire village of Chalfont told a gruesome legend about their pond. Once a young girl had waited there for a lover who never came. Wretched and distraught, she had drowned herself and, so the story went, anyone who ran three times around the pond would see the dead girl's hand pushing up through the surface of the water.

In 1931 Florence Barley 23, started working as a maid in a

big house near Chalfont. She heard the legend and laughed: 'What a silly girl!'

On September 12th Florence Barley visited her father and gave him some money. 'Give this to Mum', she said. Then she left. The next morning she was reported missing. The search had lasted five days before someone thought to check the fatal pond, where local workmen stared at a clump of dank weeds in the middle. There, protruding above the water, was a girl's hand, and beneath it was a corpse, the remains of Florence Barley.

Gone With The Wind

High wire star Karl Wallenda shamed the faint-hearted as he climbed to a wire strung 100 feet above the pavement and stretched 300 feet between two seafront hotels in San Juan, Puerto Rico. As he started his walk, the 73-year-old Wallenda shouted down, 'The wind is stronger in the street than up here.' He was halfway across when a sudden gust tossed him down to his death.

Shed a Pinta. . .

Interviewed by *Newsweek* magazine on December 20, 1976, the Mayor of San Francisco, George Moscone, admitted: 'I hate to say it, but crime is an overhead you have to pay if you want to live in the city.'

Moscone was subsequently shot dead by a disgruntled ex-policeman who burst into his office and killed the Mayor and a councilman.

Street Wise

In 1970, 78-year-old Mrs Elizabeth McClelland left her native Belfast and emigrated to Christchurch, New Zealand. She told neighbours, 'I want to avoid all the street violence.'

Mrs McClelland died in a Christchurch hospital in February 1972 after being hit over the head during a demonstration by a placard proclaiming Irish Civil Rights.

Who Needs It?

Rock drummer Keith Moon, who had once observed, 'I'm the victim of my own practical jokes', and whose incandescent drumming for The Who was echoed in the excesses of his own lifestyle, claimed in 1977: 'I think we just sort of grew out of drugs. The drugs aren't necessary now.'

Moon died of an overdose of alcohol and drugs in September 1978.

Death by Misadventure

In 1976 Mr D.H. Beenan of Auckland, New Zealand, an ardent opponent of capital punishment, was demonstrating the terrible art of hanging. The onlookers, who included his fiancée, Miss Bebe Trumper, watched as he slipped a noose around his neck, stood on a chair and remarked. 'How horrible the whole thing is.'

Mr Beenan then jumped from the chair and choked himself to death.

Dust to Dust

Lemmy Chipowe, a Zambian magician, had a special trick. For one kwacha he offered: 'Bury me alive for two and a half hours, dig me up and I'll still be breathing.'

Chipowe received his fee and lay down in a grave while the audience shovelled dirt over him. Unfortunately, when they disinterred him at the appointed time, it was found that the magician had performed his last trick.

Final Pay-Off

Once upon a time Carl Switzer played the lovable rascal 'Alfalfa', star of Saturday morning 'Our Gang' comedy films. But by 1959 success was long gone and Switzer was down on his luck. One evening, drunk and broke, he walked across a bar and grabbed someone who owed him money: 'I want that $50 you owe me and I want it now!' His creditor pulled out a pistol and shot Switzer dead.

Long Shots

Terry Kath, a member of the Chicago pop group, demonstrating a new revolver to the rest of the band in 1978. He raised the gun to his head, spoofing Russian Roulette, and laughed. 'Don't worry, it's not loaded. . .'

But Kath was wrong.

In 1893 Anthony J. Drexel III, scion of a wealthy New York family, was showing visitors the treasures of the gun room. He picked up his latest acquisition. 'Look, here's one you haven't seen before. . .'

Drexel then waved the pistol at himself, pulled the trigger and shot himself dead.

Twenty-three-year-old Benny Vincent was showing his two-year-old son how to hold his 0.22 calibre pistol. Then he showed him how to work the trigger. The boy responded, grasping the gun, and his proud father urged him: 'Now, son, pull!'

At the inquest into her husband's death, Mrs Vincent told the court that she had heard the crack of the 0.22 and turned around to see Benny on the ground, shot through the head.

Money and His Life

When, in November 1979, Manchester schoolteacher Harry Johnson, 59, won over £750,000 on the pools, he became both a national figure and a very rich man overnight. Unfortunately, Harry fell victim to a mysterious 'bug'. His wife Mabel was worried. 'He's hardly ever been sick before. I think the shock of winning so much money is just setting in.' But Harry was unperturbed. He planned to buy new cars, a new home and to sail off on the obligatory world cruise. He told his friends: 'My God, I've won all this money. I hope I'm not going to kick the bucket before I can spend some of it.'

In December 1979, barely six weeks after his famous win,

Harry Johnson suffered a heart attack and dropped dead. Said the doctor: 'Good news can sometimes be as fatal as bad for a man of his age. A shock to the system can result in death several weeks afterwards.'

L-Plates

On April 25, 1974, the Toronto *Star* reported the deaths of Mr Todd Missfield and Ms Bonnie Johnson, who died when their Cessna 150 airplane crashed into a billboard. The message on the billboard read: 'Learn to Fly'.

All Washed Up

On July 13, 1793, there was a special visitor to the home of French revolutionary leader Jean-Paul Marat. A young woman, Charlotte Corday, told Marat's suspicious companions: 'I wish to put him in a condition to render a great service to France.'

Then, as Marat sat in his tub, the girl pulled a six-inch butcher's knife from the folds of her dress and plunged it into his heart. Corday died on the scaffold four days later, but Marat never stepped from his bloody bathwater.

Fare Game

In 1972 Alfred Lewis was sitting aboard a Chicago Transit Authority bus when he noticed that he had missed his stop. The driver refused to let him off before the next stop, whereupon an enraged Lewis pulled out a pistol and screamed: 'I am going to get off this bus if I have to blast my way off!'

At this point another passenger produced *his* pistol and started shooting. Seven passengers were wounded in the shoot-out that followed, but Lewis did get off his bus – feet-first and en route for the morgue.

Never Say Die!

When Washington State's Mount St Helen started making threatening noises early in 1980, at least one person refused to worry about the rumblings coming from the dormant volcano. Harry Truman, 83 years old, had lived on the slopes of the mountain for fifty years, where he owned and ran a holiday lodge for tourists and climbers.

The media naturally converged on Mt St Helen's oldest human resident, although they lacked his fortitude when the volcano let off some exploratory sulphur streams. 'They tore away like striped-assed apes' sneered a contemptuous Harry, still felling trees around the lodge. He informed the attentive press: 'No-one knows more about this mountain than Harry.

And it don't dare blow up on him. This goddamned mountain won't blow. Scientists don't know shit from apple butter!'

When the mountain finally exploded, Harry was still defying fate. He died, along with his sixteen cats, when the mighty tide of lava obliterated his lodge.

Night of the Zombie

A popular Hungarian hypnotist was giving his standard performance in the small town of Izsak in 1936. As usual, he called for a volunteer to help with the show. A young farmer, Karoly Szani, stood up and offered himself as a subject, and he was soon deep in a trance. The hypnotist began to give him directions: 'Here is a knife. Take it. Stand up, here comes one of your enemies. You hate him because he has stolen away your sweetheart.' The farmer responded perfectly, and the hypnotist pursued his subject: 'Look out! Your foe is about to attack you! Get him!'

Szani sprang forward and stabbed viciously with the knife, thrusting it deep into the hypnotist's heart. The performer was rushed off to hospital, and poor Szani was dragged out of the trance by a local doctor. He remembered nothing.

THE END IS NIGH

The world of prophecy never fails to amaze. Predicting the end or even tomorrow is a dangerous profession. And people *pay* for this stuff!

Starry-Eyed

Frederic Davies, 'The Man the Stars Consult', predicted the events of 1974 under the headline '1974 – this year of peace and hope.'

'Prince Charles will get engaged this year, either to a Taurus or an Aquarius, with the initials JM or W'; 'the Concorde will start to get big orders'; 'if there is a general election this year, Ted Heath will be re-elected'; 'President Nixon will not resign.'

Davies ended his piece: 'I promise that 1974 will amaze you.' Him too, one might imagine.

On Election Day, February 25, 1974, in his *Evening News* column, Davies reaffirmed his choice of Heath for power. 'Edward Heath has chosen the perfect day for his re-election. The mood of the people as they go to the polls will be a genuine wish for a return to law and order . . . it is the start of the way to peaceful prosperity . . . immediate problems will be solved.'

For all his errors, Davies is nothing if not consistent. In 1978 he announced 'President Carter will be re-elected in 1980.'

You Bet!

Of course, betting on elections on the evidence of psychic predictions is a dangerous pastime. Malcolm Bessent, alumnus of the London College of Psychic Science, in 1969: 'Ed Muskie will beat Richard Nixon in 1972 election.'

Jeanne Dixon, leading American fortune-teller: 'The US will have its first woman president elected in 1980.'

And the more practical realms of journalism are little more help. Henry Fairlie, political writer for the *Spectator*, in 1980: 'Jimmy Carter will be the next President of the United States.' Alan Vaughan, science writer: 'Teddy Kennedy will be President in 1976.'

Clues to the Future

Still, such mistakes are fairly mild. They merely back the loser in a two-horse race. More dire and dreadful are the long-term prospects as variously envisaged by today's popular predictors:

Jeanne Dixon, in 1967: 'The Soviets are plotting to force, by nuclear blackmail, a Vietnam peace treaty on their own terms. They will threaten to annihilate nine US cities by means of orbiting satellites, each carrying a cluster of atomic warheads.' A sinister column, staffed by millionaires 'with tentacles reaching to London and Paris', are forming a shadow government to take over America.

Criswell, a former teacher and mortician who claims 86 per cent accuracy, has offered: 'A new Korean war by 1969; the assassination of Fidel Castro, by a woman, on August 9, 1970; the devastation of Hawaii in 1976; the return of New Mexico to the Indians in 1976; a year of massive disasters in 1977 with a new Black Death decimating the world's populations, ten months of drought, followed by floods which, among other places, will roll over New York City; in 1978 Lake Michigan will be drained for land reclamation and in late 1980 cannibals will roam freely in Pennsylvania.'

Roger Elliot, a spokesman for the Astrological Association, declared in 1971: 'I can see the blacks taking over a segment of America, by 1980 people will not be eating meat. This is

212

possibly connected with some kind of blight on the animals or the fact that they may be uneconomic to harvest. I have a horrible feeling the edible animals are not going to be alive in 1980. In thirty years we will have a TV set with which we can communicate with the dead.'

Others have warned us of Chinese nuclear strikes, civil war in the United States, the economic resurgence (in 1973) of the UK and a marriage (in 1971) for then British Prime Minister, Edward Heath. The list goes on. And so, it seems, does our appetite for such prognostications.

Judge Rutherford, an enormously popular American spiritualist of the 1920s who filled the Albert Hall on his British visit, declared: 'Millions now living will never die!'

Dreamland

The 'Dream Preacher', Maria Akerbloom, a mystic, spent her time traversing her native Finland in 1923 preaching the immediate end of the world. Her message was simple, and apocalyptic: 'Own no land or house. Save no money and do no work. None of this is of use at the end.' She was arrested later that year when the authorities began to fear that her preaching was effectively undermining large chunks of the economy and ruining many individual peasants.

Hollywood Babylon

The Advanced Adventists, some 200 followers of Mrs Margaret Rowen ('the Bride of the Lamb' and a Californian doom watcher) waited eagerly on February 6, 1925, for the promised Armageddon. Mrs Rowen, who enjoyed regular 'celestial visions', had written: 'If Christ does not appear to meet his 144,000 faithful shortly after midnight on February 6th or 7th, it means that my calculations, based on the Bible, must be revised.'

One of her favoured few, Robert Reidt of Patchogue, NY, went to a hilltop with his wife and children, a local schoolteacher and the village idiot to shout 'Gabriel, oh Gabriel, we're ready!!' The last day, according to Reidt, would feature the arrival of the 'Lord on earth' in Hollywood, to which paradise 'everyone of his little flock will be transported, possibly on a cloud'. There, amidst the faithful, 'a musical programme will be given by the angels, and then the earthly brides, bridesmaids and guests will be taken on high.' Those who rejected Mrs Rowen would all die, although exactly how was not specified.

Another fan, Joseph Gammel of College View, Nebraska, modified Reidt's scenario. The Lord might not appear quite as scheduled . . . 'He will pause at some planets en route, to make arrangements for the reception of the saints he plans to take with him.'

It would appear that He's still making plans.

Four No-Trumps

William Alexander Miller started studying the Bible – in particular the Books of Daniel and Revelations – around 1831. The former farmer and atheist then announced: 'The world will be destroyed by fire on April 3, 1843.' Sceptics were less cynical after the appearance of shooting stars in 1833 and a massive comet a decade later. The New York *Herald* actually published Miller's prediction. Come April, Millerite fanatics were massing for the End.

The most devoted, believing that the dead would arrive in heaven first, began murdering their relatives and then killing themselves. This slaughter was in some cases extended to those who refused to become converts.

On April 3, as thousands waited on a New England hilltop, a ghastly sound filled their ears, but this apparent last trumpet was then found to be caused by the local village idiot blowing a large horn. And that was it for April 3rd, other than the unfortunate fractures sustained by a Millerite who tried to ascend to glory by means of the turkey wings attached to his shoulders.

Miller, unmoved by the world's continuance, moved the

last day to July 7th. He also continued to produce large numbers of white ascension robes – the expensive but recommended garb in which to approach the Apocalypse.

On July 7th nothing happened, although this time many families had dug special mass graves for themselves and were waiting patiently inside them. Miller put out a new date: March 21, 1844. Yet again the world survived. This time, unwilling to make themselves yet more coffins, many acolytes sat around in convenient graveyards. But once more Miller had failed them.

A new date was predicted: October 22nd. This time, after another peaceful night, Miller's 100,000 strong followers fragmented and deserted. Miller himself spent the next five years making speeches – financed, no doubt, by the substantial profits he had amassed selling all those ascension robes. He died, aged 67, in 1849.

Water Wings

'For £3000, you can reserve a seat to watch the Second Coming of Christ across the waters of Sydney Harbour.' Thus the suckers were gulled yet again, this time by one 'Bishop' Leadbetter, leader of an allegedly 100,000-strong worldwide sect called 'The Order of the Star in the East'. Leadbetter's Order worked along strictly business lines, extracting funds from the aspirant faithful through 1927.

The 'Bishop's' promise was that Christ was due back soon and would appear walking across the Heads, the passage of the Pacific Ocean into Sydney Harbour. He brought a ramshackle house overlooking the harbour, greatly enlarged it, and constructed an amphitheatre to seat the multitudes. Apart from the £3000 reservation fee, latecomers were offered seats for a sum commensurate with their station in life.

Labour of Love

Gladys Spearman-Cook, writing in the *Occult Gazette*, December 1968: 'Theocratic Government is the Aquarian Fulfillment. . . Yes, Harold Wilson is going to pull through to see another successful election, for Harold Wilson was NOT chosen by the people to be discarded when they so desired, but placed into office by those Great Divinities to carry out a MIGHTY task requiring honesty and sincerity. He was given the task against the EVILS set up and instilled by Tory Governments in these past decades and is the only Man that these Greater Powers can trust. . . As the Pharoah Amenhotep III he brought dynamic peace and wisdom to Egypt. Now he must fulfill his destiny and bring Britain to being the spiritual prototype for the World CONTROL OF THE EARTH. It can no longer be left in the hands of warmongers and mad scientists, or it would have been utterly destroyed. The mighty hierarchical powers will now over-shadow the Labour Government and guide it along its spiritual path of TRUE UNDERSTANDING of freedom, equality and peace. . . Vote Labour for a new world of peace and spiritual brotherhood!!'

Wilson lost the next election, in 1970. Afterwards he moaned: 'But I thought that everyone *wanted* an election. . .'

Serf's Up

Johannes Stoeffler, 16th-century German astrologer at Tubingen University, claimed: 'The world will end by a giant flood on February 20, 1524.' Unwilling to ignore such learned advice, thousands of peasants constructed wooden arks and took to the River Rhine in an attempt to emulate Noah. As it happened, Germany was hit by torrential storms on the relevant day and many peasants duly went to heaven, mainly because they had been afloat, a dangerous occupation on such a stormy occasion.

Although the world continued to turn the next day, Stoeffler's reputation was much enhanced, although a further prediction of disaster for 1528, at which time nothing untoward whatsoever occurred, ended his prophetic career.